T0158950

The M&M's of Life

An Encyclopedia
for Victorious Living

Dr. Jason Alvarez

WESTBOW
P R E S S®
A DIVISION OF THOMAS NELSON
& ZONDERVAN

Scripture quotations are taken from the King James Version unless otherwise marked.

Scripture quotations marked (THE MESSAGE) are taken from The Message. Copyright © by Eugene H. Peterson 1993, 1994, 1995, 1996, 2000, 2001, 2002. Used by permission of NavPress Publishing Group.

Scripture quotations marked (AMP) are taken from the Amplified® Bible. Copyright © 2015 by The Lockman Foundation. Used by permission. www.Lockman.org

Scripture quotations marked (AMPC) are taken from the Amplified® Bible (AMPC). Copyright © 1954, 1958, 1962, 1964, 1965, 1987 by The Lockman Foundation. Used by permission. www.Lockman.org

Scripture quotations marked (ICB) are taken from the International Children's Bible®. Copyright © 1986, 1988, 1999 by Thomas Nelson. Used by permission. All rights reserved.

Scripture quotations marked (ERV) are taken from The Holy Bible: Easy-To-Read Version. Copyright © 2001 by World Bible Translation Center, Inc. and used by permission.

Scripture quotations marked (NKJV) are taken from the New King James Version®. Copyright © 1982 by Thomas Nelson. Used by permission. All rights reserved.

WestBow Press books may be ordered through booksellers or by contacting:

WestBow Press
A Division of Thomas Nelson & Zondervan
1663 Liberty Drive
Bloomington, IN 47403
www.westbowpress.com
1 (866) 928-1240

Because of the dynamic nature of the Internet, any web addresses or links contained in this book may have changed since publication and may no longer be valid. The views expressed in this work are solely those of the author and do not necessarily reflect the views of the publisher, and the publisher hereby disclaims any responsibility for them.

Any people depicted in stock imagery provided by Thinkstock are models, and such images are being used for illustrative purposes only. Certain stock imagery © Thinkstock.

ISBN: 978-1-5127-9621-6 (sc)
ISBN: 978-1-5127-9622-3 (hc)
ISBN: 978-1-5127-9620-9 (e)

Library of Congress Control Number: 2017911231

Print information available on the last page.

WestBow Press rev. date: 07/28/2017

Table of Contents

Acknowledgments

Special thanks to my amazing wife, my dear friend Bishop Gerald Loyd, Bettye Blackston, Rev. Fred Rodriguez, our brilliant designer Ashley Cheatham, Yuriy Boyechko, Julio Vitolo, Naimah Ward, and to the tender mercy and amazing grace of my living Savior and Lord Jesus Christ.

Chapter 1

The First M—
The Mind

Your mind is the doorway and entrance into your thought life.

You might say, "I know that." Yet there are many people who don't, and for many years, I can honestly say that I was one of them! Do you know that I went to church Sunday after Sunday, but I never heard a preacher tell me that my thoughts had anything to do with my life?

No One Told Me

No one ever told me that if I was presented with a thought that wasn't correct, or that was contrary to the will of God for my life, I didn't have to keep entertaining it. Rather, I could put a stop to it. I didn't know that!

I was never made aware that God Almighty had made me the gatekeeper of my mind, and that I was responsible for what I let in or kept out of my thought life.

You see, no one—and I mean no one—ever told me that my mind could become the devil's playground if I allowed it to be. I didn't know that the mind was the battlefield—the great arena where personal victories are either won or lost. No, sir. I honestly believed, for all those years, that I had to put up with whatever thoughts were invading my mind, without ever doing a thing about them. I'm telling you, I had no idea that I could even choose my own thoughts.

Then one day, I heard someone ask, "Are you aware that you will always move in the direction of your most dominant thought?" I said no, I wasn't aware of it. Well, this person went on to point out to me how critical this was—and that even the Bible itself teaches us that as a man thinks in his heart and mind (the Hebrew says), so does he become. *Bam!*

The moment I heard it, I knew that this was exactly what had happened to me. I thought, *No wonder my life is such a mess.* Immediately, I saw how ignorant I had been of the devil's devices, and like the Bible says, I was definitely perishing for a lack of knowledge.

I had no clue that God had given me my mind to serve me and not to rule me. I didn't realize that He intended for me to be in control of it rather than my mind being in control of me. And the sad thing is that, although I had gone to church for years, no one ever told me that God had left it all up to me to bring into captivity *every thought* to the obedience of Christ—or better yet, to bring every thought chained to the foot of Calvary.

Somehow, I thought that God would take care of all the craziness that was going on in my mind on His own, without me doing a thing about it, just as long as I kept loving Jesus. The truth is that I kept loving Jesus all right, but nothing ever changed until I began binding the devil up and breaking his power over my mind.

Now here are two important truths concerning your mind that you ought to know.

Truth Number 1

Listen to me: Since the time you were a child, you have been molded into the person you are today thanks to whatever you had been feeding your mind.

But for many years, I had no clue of that. Neither was I aware that the spirit of your mind, which is the sum total of all your thoughts, is what created your inner mental constitution, your belief system, your moral compass, and your behavior.

And so I lived my life out of negative input, without knowing the implications of it.

Truth Number 2

The good news is that it didn't take long before I began to see that the enemy's main attack was against my mind, and that it was all up to me to learn to do something about it. At first, when I didn't know any better, it almost seemed impossible because his attacks on my mind were relentless! For example, I remember being attacked daily with constant thoughts of discouragement and fear. Then at other times, it was severe thoughts of despair and depression. But his all-time favorite was the thought of giving up. He knew that if he succeeded in getting me to give up, then I would not be here today, having and enjoying this amazing life that God has so graciously given me. He knew that I would not be doing all of the incredible things that God has graced me and privileged me to do so far—and the *best is yet to come*!

Are you aware that ever since the Garden of Eden, not only has Satan's method of operation against humanity been limited by God so that Satan cannot use his angelic powers against us, but that even today those exact methods remain the same?

If you study the Bible, you will learn that this is exactly the same method Satan used to wear out Samson. The writer informs us that when Delilah first approached Samson about the secret to his strength, he refused to tell her. However, when Delilah pressed him daily (or bombarded his mind day after day) with her words (or fiery darts aimed at his mind) and urged him, Samson was vexed to death—or like we say in the streets, she beat him down.

This is why you must learn to resist the devil at the onset of his temptations and bind up those thoughts in Jesus's name. Or else, just like Samson, after a while you will become weary and faint in your mind. The truth is that you can't stop thoughts from knocking on your mind's door. However, it's totally up to you which ones you let in and keep out! So I urge you—whenever you are tempted to become discouraged and give up, learn to rise up quickly against the enemy's onslaught and say, "No, devil, I bind you and break your power over my mind right now in Jesus's mighty name!"

Then quickly replace those negative thoughts with one of the promises of God that fits your situation, and give God praise.

Now let me tell you what I've done, and I encourage you to do the same. I have put up a big sign in the realm of the spirit that says, "Devil, keep out! And yes, Satan, this means you!"

Don't Quit!

I once heard the story of a garage sale the devil was having. In this garage sale, the devil was selling many, many tools. But there was one tool in particular that looked old and totally worn out, yet this was the one item he was asking the most for.

So one of the buyers asked him, "Why so much money for this old and worn-out tool?"

The devil answered, "Because this is the one tool I've used more than all the others, and it has also gotten me the best results."

You may wonder what the tool is. Is it divorce, murder, adultery, greed, or maybe regret? No, his number-one tool is the temptation to quit. No wonder Daniel 7:25 teaches us that the devil's great objective in the last days is to wear out the saints of the most high God. And trust me, he is doing a pretty good job. This is why so many ministers are leaving the ministry and why so many churches are closing their doors.

A Vision

Now let me share with you a mini-vision I had many years ago that really helped me along this line. In the vision, I saw a man and a woman who had never met, and they were simply standing at a bus stop next to each other—when suddenly I saw the man boldly put his hand on the woman's shoulder and gently begin to rub it. Then the Lord asked me, "What do you think would happen if that woman doesn't quickly remove his hand and let him know that she doesn't want him doing that?" I answered, "I imagine the man would just get bolder and bolder and more aggressive." He said, "You're right!"

He went on to teach me: "Here's the deal: In the realm of the spirit, the way the devil puts his filthy hands on you is through thoughts. And unless you resist him at the onset and bind up those thoughts in my name, there is no telling where these attacks will end."

Are you aware that divorce begins with a thought? I don't know about you, but when my wife and I were having big problems, the thought of divorce must have crossed my mind thousands of times. Thank God, however, that when I was young in the Lord I heard Prophet David Minor recall someone asking him a question concerning divorce. "Dr. Minor, do you believe in divorce?" was the query, to which he answered, "Murder, maybe ... Divorce, never!"

Relax, it's just a joke! All kidding aside, the real truth is that if I had a dime for every time I got discouraged and was tempted to give up, I'd probably be rich by now—and most likely, so would you!

How about Murder?

Let's say that somebody hurts you, mistreats you, or takes advantage of you, and as a result you refuse to forgive this person, because perhaps the pain is too great. Immediately, the spirit of anger will do everything within his power to get a foothold in your life by attacking your mind with thoughts of anger and revenge. If you don't rise up quickly and put a stop to this (anger) in the thought realm, then the seed of anger will soon give way to a root of bitterness.

And if that bitterness is not dealt with and uprooted, it will give birth to hatred, and hatred, if not diffused, dealt with, and repented of, can turn into murder.

Now here's the amazing thing. It all started with a thought that was not bound, dealt with, and repented of. Again, the great lesson here is that if we will put a stop to sin in the thought realm, it will *never* turn into a deed.

What about Suicide?

Are you aware that suicide begins with a thought? You know, as I ponder the loss of a famous gentleman who recently hanged himself to death at the age of sixty-three, I can't help but feel that this message could have helped him. Not only him, but scores of people who have allowed this wicked spirit of suicide to push them over the edge with thoughts to taking their own lives. Even in my own town, just recently, a beautiful fifteen-year-old girl who had so much going for her and so much to live for made the mistake of listening to the devil's lies and wound up taking her own life. I've got to tell you, man, my heart really goes out to these precious people and their families, so much so that this is really one of the main reasons I'm writing this book. My heart-felt prayer is that it will help and rescue many from this hopeless path of destruction, in Jesus's name.

Are you even aware that the spirit of suicide tried to talk Jesus into jumping off of the pinnacle of the temple? Oh yes, he did! But Jesus didn't fall for it; instead, He pulled out the Sword of the Spirit, pointed it at the devil, and said, "It is written, thou shall not tempt the Lord thy God." And with that, He whipped the devil and sent him off running for his life.

Now let me ask you a question: Have you ever been tempted with thoughts of suicide? I have! It happened once, when I traveled with Evangelist R.W. Shambach. I remember stepping out onto a small balcony in the tenth floor of our hotel, when suddenly, I clearly heard a voice say to me, "Jason, why don't you do your wife and family a favor and just jump off?"

You see, at this time my wife and I were having great problems, and our life was extremely difficult. You know what they say: "The closest you'll ever get to hell, without really going there, is a bad marriage." Man, that's a mouthful. But I can firmly assert that it is true, because I have been there.

But today, my marriage is heaven on earth. You can read all about it when you get to the chapter on marriage. At any rate, when Satan tried to get me to jump off the balcony, instead of letting him torment me with his thoughts, I quickly rose up and said to him, "Devil, *it is written* in Jesus's name. Jump off, yourself! Haha!" And with that, I knew I had shut him up and shut him down, because I didn't hear another peep from him again.

But honestly, there was a time in my life when my mind was fried, always under attack, constantly being tormented with insecurities, the fear of failure, and thoughts of giving up. I didn't think I had much of a chance of making it. But God!

That's why I'll never cease to celebrate what I call my independence day, the day I made the quality decision (from which there was no turning back) to daily renew my mind to the Word of God and also to read other healthy material. I'm not going to tell you that it was easy, because it wasn't. But man, was it ever worth it! Because today, I am not the same person I used to be. The main reason for this supernatural metamorphosis in my life is the way I now think and perceive life. I am a witness that you will never be depressed and become hopeless if you're entertaining healthy thoughts and thinking the thoughts of God. So if you have been victimized by your own thoughts and the attack of the enemy, I can assure you that if you dare to do what I did, the same can happen with you, because God is no respecter of persons.

Today, I am so grateful to God for what I call a (double portion of) second chance, meaning that when I got saved, it was my spirit that was born again, or got a second chance, but my mind still had to be renewed … changed … metamorphosed.

But now that my mind is being continuously renewed and metamorphosed through the Word of God and healthy thoughts, I am a new man. Not just in my spirit, where I became a new creation when I was born again, but also in my mind.

You see, I have discovered that when you start thinking right, talking right, and acting right, right things start happening.

Please hear me. You cannot get beyond your own thoughts because where the mind goes, "the man follows." This is why, it is very possible for a person who really loves God and has a new heart (through the new birth) to still have an old mind. By that I mean a mind that has not been renewed by the Word of God.

This is why it's vital for you, once you're born again, not to stop there, but to dare to take the next step and begin the process of renewing your mind through the Word of God. This is what I call "putting on the mind of Christ."

Did you know the Bible teaches us that wrong thoughts are the root cause for a troubled mind? Consider the case of King Belteshazzar found in Daniel 5:6 KJV "Then the king's countenance was changed, and *his thoughts troubled him*, so that the joints of his loins were loosed, and his knees smote one against another." Wow! Isn't that amazing? So if you're troubled, check with your mind and see what it's been thinking about or entertaining.

On the other hand, Isaiah 26:3 offers you a key to victory: God said, "I will keep you in perfect and complete peace." In other words, God is saying, ["This is what I will do. But here's the condition, an "if …" *If what?* "If you do your part and keep your mind fixed and stayed on me."] Now what does that mean? It means to think on these things. What things? Whatsoever things are true, whatsoever things are honest, whatsoever things are just, whatsoever things are pure, whatsoever things are lovely, whatsoever things are of good report; if there be any virtue, and if there be any praise, think on these things (or fix your mind on the Word and His promises)

Philippians 4:8, and the God of Peace shall be with you and will keep you in perfect and complete peace. ...

The Bible also teaches that one wrong thought can keep you from your miracle!

In 2 Kings 5:10 and 11, we read:

> "And Elisha sent a messenger unto him, saying, Go and wash in Jordan seven times [signifying complete obedience], and thy flesh shall come again to thee, and thou shalt be clean".

> But Naaman was wroth, and went away, and said, "Behold, I THOUGHT, He will surely come out to me, and stand, and call on the name of the LORD his God, and strike his hand over the place, and recover the leper ...

> Are not Abana and Pharpar, rivers of Damascus, better than all the waters of Israel? may I not wash in them, and be clean? So he turned and went away in a rage. And his servants came near, and spake unto him, and said, My father, if the prophet had bid thee do some great thing, wouldest thou not have done it? How much rather then, when he saith to thee, Wash, and be clean? Then went he down, (or humbled himself) and dipped himself seven times in Jordan [seven times speaks of complete obedience], according to the saying of the man of God: and (Then) his flesh came again like unto the flesh of a little child, and he was clean."

Here we see that Naaman had a preconceived idea about how God should heal him, but he was wrong. Because the truth is, you can't put God in a box. Moreover, had he not humbled himself, changed his mind, and obeyed the man of God, he would have remained a leper the rest of his life and would never have experienced the miracle of healing.

I can't even begin to tell you how many times people have walked into our church with a preconceived idea of how God was supposed to heal them that day, or perform some type of a special miracle for them, only to walk away disappointed and sometimes even angry because God didn't do it exactly the way they had anticipated or imagined. So is it possible that one wrong thought or preconceived idea might be keeping you from your miracle, or your healing, your deliverance, or your financial breakthrough? Think about it: You might be just one thought away from a breakthrough! If this is the case, I suggest you get back into the Word and diligently search the scriptures until you find out for yourself, and know that you know what the Bible has to say about your specific situation. Then position yourself to receive your miracle! Your breakthrough! This is why I always say, if you think education is costly, try ignorance!

Now here is another rich nugget from my personal experience that I believe will be a great blessing to you. This revelation came to me as I was talking with a friend who looked and sounded totally out of it. When I asked her if she was all right, she responded, "Do you know what today is?" I answered no, so she said, "Forty years ago on this date, my brother died, and ever since, whenever this time comes around, I get really depressed just thinking about it. Do you know what I mean?"

I said, "Yes, I know what you mean, *but I won't let my mind go there.*" The minute I said that, I knew God had given me another key to victory in dealing with my thought life.

You see, before this simple revelation, my mind would take me places that I sometimes found very difficult to come back from. For example, sometimes my mind would take me back to a missed opportunity or something I had greatly regretted doing in the past. And before long, I would find myself plunging back into such a deep state of depression that would often take me days and sometimes weeks to come out of.

At other times, my mind would literally take me back to places where I had been betrayed and taken advantage of, so much so, that a sudden spirit of anger and hatred would get such a hold of me that for days I would be like a ticking time bomb, ready to go off. Thank God I'm free!

This is why now, whenever the enemy attempts to take control of me by attacking my mind with thoughts that try to take me places I know I shouldn't be going,

I immediately rise up and say, "No, devil, no, no, no! *I won't let my mind go there, in Jesus's name!*" And off he goes! Listen to me, I can't even begin to tell you what a huge blessing this simple revelation has been to me, and now, I pass it on to *you. Work it!*

To close this chapter, let me share a story about a man from India who found a baby elephant out in the wild. The man somehow managed to bring the animal back to the small hut where he lived. He then anchored a long peg into the ground, found a fifteen-foot rope, and tied the elephant's foot to it to keep it from running away. For a while, the baby elephant continually attempted to do just that. But every time he did, the rope around his foot would jerk him back and hurt him. So after a while, the baby elephant just stopped. Now here's the amazing thing: Although this elephant is now full-grown and has the power and ability to uproot that little peg in the ground with the smallest effort, *he won't,* because in his mind, *he still thinks he can't!*

So know this! That whatever had you bound in the past, can no longer keep you bound! You are now a free and can-do person through Jesus Christ!

And I prophesy, you can now break free, break loose, break out, break through, and conquer your world in Jesus's name! *Get ready for a new you!*

Chapter 2

The Second M— The Mouth

A man's belly shall be satisfied with the fruit of his mouth, and with the increase of his lips shall he be fed. Death and life are in the power of the tongue: and they that love it shall eat the fruit thereof.

—Proverbs 18:20–21 (KJV)

My Greatest Christmas Present

Let me begin by sharing with you the story of the greatest Christmas present I have ever been given. The gift was a cassette by Kenneth Copeland titled "The Power of the Tongue." Can you imagine, on a Christmas day, the one and only present you receive from your wife is a teaching cassette? Wow! Honestly, I thought she was crazy. The truth is I was quite insulted.

However, little did I know that this cassette would turn out to be the greatest Christmas gift I would ever receive from anyone. God used it to radically change the course of my life. I will never forget the feeling I had as I listened to the message for the first time. I could not believe what I was hearing! I thought, *I have known for a long time that my mind was a mess, but Lord, I didn't realize that it was my mouth that was digging my own grave!*

Take, for instance, Proverbs 18:21, in which Solomon teaches us that death and life are in the power of the tongue. Notice that he does not say that death and life are in the devil's power or even in God's power, but in the power of your tongue and my tongue. In all the years of my journey, nobody but nobody had ever told me that!

You see, before I was saved, I had learned from eastern religions that the mind was the part of man that possessed almost infinite power. But as I began to receive insight into scriptures such as this, I soon discovered that there was a huge difference between thoughts and words.

For example, when God Almighty got ready to create His world, He didn't think it into existence. He spoke it into existence. (Read Genesis 1:1–3.)

Again, notice he didn't stand there with his eyes closed and his hands stretched, straining like they do in the *Star Wars* movies to somehow think it into existence (using mind power). No, He used words! "Let there be light and there was light." In a flash, I received this amazing revelation.

You see, it is the mind that's the seedbed or womb for ideas and plans to be conceived. But it is words and words alone that possess the ability and power to create.

Amazingly enough, I also discovered that thoughts do have presence. Oh yes, they do. You can be in the same room with people who don't really like one another or get along with each other, and without a word ever being spoken, the tension and atmosphere can be so thick that you can cut it with a knife. And the reason for this is because thoughts do have presence.

However, as we have already seen, it is words that possess creative power.

No wonder God himself tells us, "I create the fruit of the lips …" (Isa. 57:19). In other words, God works with the material (or words) you put in His hands.

Let me ask you a question: What have you been saying with your mouth? What kind of material have you been putting in His hands? Are you pleased and happy with the results? If you're not, here's a life-changing principle that I often share with people who are frustrated and dissatisfied with their journey in life. I tell them, "If you don't like your life, change it!" Without fail, they always ask me, "How?" Then I always challenge them, "Start with your words!"

This change doesn't happen overnight. But think about it, the mess you may be in today didn't happen overnight either. Trust me, it will take time and hard work, but the good news is that it's possible! And it's definitely worth it.

Now here are the two main scriptures God used to give me this simple revelation: Hebrews 11:3 and Psalm 50:19.

Framing Your World

1. Through faith we understand that the worlds were *framed* by the Word of God. Notice that God used words *to frame the world* in Hebrews 11:3.
2. hen, in Psalm 50:19, David, the sweet psalmist wrote, "Thou givest thy mouth to evil, and thy tongue 'frames' deceit." Wow! Notice he says it is your mouth that "frames" deceit.

Here I began to discover that the tongue was the instrument used by both God and man to frame evil or good, success or failure, life or death, plenty or lack. Suddenly I realized that everything that was happening in my life didn't just happen by chance; it had somehow or another been framed by words. Therefore, if I expected things to change, I was going to have to use my words to do something about it.

So little by little I began framing a new world for myself. One brick ... one word at a time. A little bit here and a little bit there. And before long, I saw my life go from death to life, from poverty to wealth, from sickness to health, and from misery and defeat to joy and victory. And so yes, I am a witness that if you will dare work the Word, the Word will work with your world. Now here's a truth that I strongly believe needs to be reinforced inside of you. The mind is always the place of conception. It is the seedbed or womb for ideas and plans to be conceived, but it is always the tongue that has the ability to frame, bring forth, and give substance to that plan. I'll say it to you again: If you don't like your life, change it!

Now, in most cases, a new vocabulary will be required. First, let's start with Albert Einstein's definition of *insanity,* which basically says that you can't keep doing and saying the same thing over and over again and expect to have different results. Right? Well, that applies here as well.

If you want things to change in your life, the first thing you must do is to discipline your mouth to speak the Word of Promise (God's Word) in the face of all opposition, no matter what it looks like and no matter what it feels like. (This is called *discipline.*)

The second thing is that you must learn to focus on the promise and not the problem. In other words, *keep your eyes on the prize!* And how do you do that?

Do what Hebrews 12 says in the Amplified Bible.

Look away from all that would distract you unto Jesus (or unto the promise).

It goes on to say that "He (Jesus), for the joy [of obtaining the prize] that was set before Him, endured the cross". Heb. 12:2 AMPC Can you see it? You must have something worthwhile in front of you, something worth reaching for and fighting for—something that will ultimately bring you such joy that you will never ever even consider the thought of giving in, giving out, or giving up until you have fully obtain the prize and walk away with the promise.

Now, if you do this (not just talk about it, but do it!), I'm sure it will shoot such adrenaline into your soul that no devil or circumstance will ever be able to stop you from obtaining anything you set your sights on. Wow! Wow! Wow!

Thirdly, after having done all, stand and praise God by faith in advance for the victory! Don't wait for the walls to fall down. Shout now! That's right, shout now, and give God the glory, because your Jericho walls are coming down.

Remember, we walk by faith and not by sight!

Here's another amazing scripture about the power of the tongue that has played a huge role in my life: "Behold, we put bits in the horses' mouths, that they may obey us ..." and as a result, we control their whole body.

This is simply saying that, in the same way a small bit can bring a large horse under subjugation and turn him in the desired direction, even so the tongue, when used correctly, will do the same for us.

James goes on to say, "Behold also the ships, which though they be so great, and are driven of fierce winds, yet are they turned about with a very small helm, whithersoever the governor listeth." James 3:4 (KJV) This scripture revealed to me that even a large ship (which is a type of our life and all that pertains to it), although it is often driven by fierce winds and raging seas, can still be turned in the desired direction by a very small helm, which is our tongue. The question is, *how big is your want? How badly do you want change?*

Are You Aware That

God gave you a mouth to multiply what's in your mind!

God gave you a mouth to conquer what's in your mind!

God gave you a mouth to be a weapon against your mind and what the mind invents!

God gave you a mouth to prophesy to the four winds and as a result change the course of your life and accomplish the impossible? Now, *do it in Jesus's name!*

I know, that some of you in your present situation might be saying, "Oh, Pastor Jason, you just don't know what I'm going through." I understand that, and I'm sure you're going through a lot. However, never ever leave God out of the equation. Never ever forget that with God, all things are possible! And to him or her who believes, nothing shall be called impossible. Right now, I believe, God has a miracle with your name on it!

Listen to me! I'm a witness! God can turn the ship of your life around—he did it for me. And I strongly believe that He will also do it for you!

Now rise up, in the name of Jesus, and take charge of your ship, which is your life.

Go ahead and boldly grab hold of that small rudder (which is your tongue) and begin to speak and prophesy God's Word over your life and situation. And don't you dare stop until you fully arrive at your new desired destination in Jesus's name. I prophesy over you right now: "It shall be done in Jesus's name!"

Trapped by Your Words

As I continued on my journey with the Lord, Solomon began teaching me that it was my words that were ensnaring me and holding me captive, and not so much my situations. In Proverbs 6:2, he said, "Thou art snared with the words of thy mouth, thou art taken captive with the words of thy mouth". The ICB translation says it this way: "You might get trapped by what you say; you might be caught by your own words." By then, I knew I desperately needed to learn how to gain control over my mouth, because although I really wanted to, I still didn't know exactly how to do it.

Funny, but I remember the first New Year's Eve service after I got saved, it was right before the clock struck midnight. I recall saying, "Today, when the clock strikes twelve, I'm going to turn over a new leaf. Oh yes, from today on, I'm only going to speak good words, wholesome words, words that lift, heal, and bless. Yes Lord, from today on my mouth will only speak Your Word." And I meant every word of it.

But amazingly enough, before long, I found myself unable to keep my tongue from speaking the complete opposite. So I asked the Lord, "Why can't I bring my tongue under control even though I have such a great desire to do so and therefore please You?"

This is what Jesus said to me: "Son, when it comes to speaking My Word, desire alone is not enough. For didn't I say in Matthew 12:34 that out of the abundance of the heart the mouth speaks? That's why desire alone is not enough. So if you truly desire to speak My Words, you must first learn to pump your heart full of them."

The Mouth

With that, He said, "What do you think would happen if you were to fill a big plastic jug with water and afterward crush it with your feet? What do you think would come out of it?"

I answered, "Whatever the jug was filled with."

He responded, "You're right, and it is no different with your heart! That's why you must daily pump your heart full of My Word, so that when difficult situations arise and life's pressures try to crush you, what's in your heart is what will automatically come out of your mouth without you even thinking about it."

Man, I saw it! How could I possibly be speaking words of life and faith-filled words in the midst of the challenges and pressures of life when my heart was filled with wrong, ungodly words? (Now here's what I'm talking about!)

Let's say you are driving your car, and somebody abruptly cuts you off and gives you the finger (you know what I'm talking about). Right then and there is when you discover whether your heart is full of the Word or full of something else. Because immediately, if your heart is not full of the Word, the thing that will come flying out of your mouth will not be pleasant or godly—and trust me, I discovered firsthand that it takes a while before many of us are able to pass this test. So this is why we must daily, and without interruption, feed on the Word and pump our hearts full of His Word. Once he gave me the key, I started doing my very best to obey him, and I haven't stopped yet.

But as the journey continued, I soon discovered that the old saying "Sticks and stones might break my bones, but words will never hurt me" was a big, big lie!

Because later on, in Proverbs 12:18, I discovered that there are people whose words are like the piercings of a sword, always cutting and wounding. Then, in Psalm 57:4, David wrote, "My enemies use their tongue as a sharp sword." (To wound and cut.)

Then, in Psalm 52:4 (ERV), we read these amazing words: "You and your lying tongue love to hurt people." Wow! Wow! Wow!

Now can you see it? "This is why I plead with you." If you have been using your tongue as a cutting and destructive instrument, please stop right now!

Because I strongly believe that many of the unexplained troubles in our lives could very well be tied to, and for the most part be the results of, the hurtful and destructive words that we have spoken with our mouths. Now, if this is for you, I pray you will receive it. If it's not, just set it aside.

Do what Kenneth Hagin used to say, "Just eat the hay and throw away the sticks." As for me, when I received this revelation, I immediately began praying, "Father, please forgive me for using my tongue to hurt, cut, and wound people. Have mercy on me, Lord, and teach and empower me to use my tongue from now on, to lift, heal, and set the captives free in Jesus's name!" I strongly urge you to do the same.

The Word as Your Covering

Next, I want to teach you how to use the Word of God to cover and protect yourself, just in case someone has cursed you or is using witchcraft and voodoo against you. If you had told me this years ago, I would have thought you were crazy, because I didn't really believe in that kind of stuff. However, things changed drastically because of an experience I had with my infant son Joshua.

We had adopted Joshua upon birth from a crack-addicted mother. When he was seventeen days old, out of the clear blue, he suddenly got sick and had to be rushed to the hospital. After a couple of days of him being there and the doctors not being able to find out what was wrong, God in his mercy clearly spoke to me and said, "Son, the problem with Joshua is not so much physical as it is spiritual. Someone in that crack house has unleashed the spirit of witchcraft on him. This is why the doctors are totally in the dark and don't know what to do. So if you want Joshua to be healed, you will first have to attack and defeat this thing in the spirit, before you can get your breakthrough."

Man, I had never heard of such a thing before. So I began praying and fasting, binding and loosing in Jesus's name according to Matthew 17:21. In this passage, Jesus teaches His disciples, "… this kind can only come out by prayer and fasting." And to my utter amazement, after a few days of doing this, the enemy's power was broken over him. Suddenly, the light came on, and the doctors finally discovered what was wrong with him. As a result, Joshua was instantly healed and came home. Thank God he's been well ever since and is presently on fire for God.

This is why now, every day of my life, I use these scriptures as preventive medicine and a divine covering for myself and family against the works of the devil. Let me show you how I do it: I simply open my mouth and boldly confess, according to the words of Isaiah 54:17, "Satan, no weapon that is formed against me, my family or ministry shall prosper or succeed in Jesus' name, and Every Tongue that shall rise up against us in judgment, I condemn in Jesus' Name. I say you're brought to naught and rendered helpless, I say you're proven to be in the wrong and your assignment against us is cancelled in the Mighty name of Jesus.

For this is my heritage as the servant of the Lord, and their righteousness is of me, smith the Lord of hosts! Amen!"

Here is another scripture that I always pray to cover myself and my family with:

> Daily, I boldly confess, Satan, it is written and now on record. God Frustrates and Disappoints your devices, so that your hands cannot perform their enterprises against me and my family, I say you meet with darkness in the daytime and you grope in the noonday as in the nighttime and all your plans, and all of your strategies are of none effect to work against me, my family and ministry, in Jesus' mighty name. Amen! Job 5:12–14

Let me also encourage you to daily plead the blood of Jesus over yourself, and family. And remember! *No weapon!*

Now here's another amazing revelation. Would you believe that the Bible teaches us that we have the same spirit of faith as King David and the great Apostle Paul? Oh yes! Paul writes, "We having the same spirit of faith, according as it is written, I believed, and *therefore have I spoken*; we also believe and *therefore speak*" (2 Cor. 4:13). Here, Paul is quoting King David, who declares the same thing in Psalm 116:10. These scriptures taught me that faith is *voice activated*. This is why, whenever you speak the Word of God in faith, the spirit of faith is released. And when the spirit of faith is released and injects the atmosphere, *miracles happen!*

JJ's Miracle Story

I'll never forget JJ's miracle story. I was sitting in my sanctuary all by myself, praying, when suddenly, I received a frantic phone call from one of our members who was pregnant. She was sobbing uncontrollably and said, "Pastor, the doctor just examined me and told me my baby is dead in my womb!" My adamant response was,

"No, we're not going to receive this evil report! Right now, we're going to pray, release our faith and believe God for a miracle!"

So I began prophesying to the four winds according to Ezekiel 37:9–10. I remember prophesying, "Come from the four winds oh breath and breathe resurrection life into this baby in my sister's womb right now, in Jesus' name!" After I prophesied, I began to say, "Thank you, Jesus. Thank you, Jesus …" And within a few minutes, to our utter amazement, the baby began to kick inside her and came back to life. Well, I don't need to tell you that we both had a Holy Ghost fit! Today, her child is twenty-nine years old and strong as a bull, and God Almighty is doing great things in his life. To God be all the glory!

Here's the good news: Our "God is no respecter of persons" Acts 10:34. What He has done for me, He will do for you, and what He will do for you, He will also do for another, if we just dare believe. This incident clearly taught me that whenever you speak the Word of God in faith, or boldly decree a thing, the spirit of faith is released. And once the spirit of faith is released and invades the atmosphere, *miracles happen!*

That day I discovered that unless you're willing to do the ridiculous, you will never experience the miraculous.

By the way, here is the scripture I used to pray and prophesy over JJ:

> Then said he unto me, prophesy unto the wind, prophesy, son of man, and say to the wind, thus saith the Lord God; come from the four winds, o breath, and breathe upon these slain, that they may live. So I prophesied as he commanded me, and the breath came into them, and they lived, and stood up upon their feet, an exceeding great army. Ezek. 37:9-10

This is why I strongly believe that prayer, praise, and prophecy—what I call the holy trinity of power—is what many times releases miracles and God's unlimited potential for future possibilities in our lives. *Now do it!*

Finally, here are some of the prayers I pray daily that I believe will help you tremendously and greatly bless your life:

1. Father, I thank You, that You are hiding me in the secret of Your presence from the pride of man and keeping me secretly in a pavilion from the strife of tongues in Jesus' name.

2. Father, I praise You, by faith in advance for teaching me to prosper and leading me in the best paths for my life in Jesus' name.

3. Father, I praise You for giving me the power, the ability, the knowledge, the credit, the favor, the wisdom, and the means to get wealth so that Your covenant could be established here on the earth in Jesus' name.

4. Heavenly Father, I thank you for daily loading me with benefits!

5. Father, today I thank You for forgiving me all my iniquities, healing all my diseases, redeeming my life from destruction, crowning me with tender mercies and loving kindness, and satisfying my mouth with good things so that my youth is being renewed like the eagle, in Jesus' name.

6. Almighty God, today I boldly confess, I will live and not die and declare the works of the Lord.

7. Father, I thank You that with long life you satisfy me and show me Your salvation.

8. Father, I pray, let all the lying lips be put to silence which speak grievous things proudly and contemptuously against us, O God. Let all those who hate the church and who seek to do me, and my family harm be confounded and turned backward. Father, let them be brought to utter shame and

let them cover themselves with their own confusion as with a mantle. Abba Father, let them be as the chaff before the wind and let the angel of the Lord chase them. Let their way be dark and slippery and let the angel of the Lord persecute them. Father, let them all hang on the gallows they have built for us and fall into the pit they have dug for us, and let their names be erased from remembrance once and for all in Jesus' name. Father, today I praise You and thank You for daily loading me and my family with benefits and protecting us from all harm, dangers, accidents, and freakish things, in Jesus' name, amen!

9. Here is a prayer releasing Abraham's blessings over my family and me:
   Father, it is written, Christ has redeemed me from the curse of the broken law by becoming a curse for me, for it is written cursed is every man that hangs on a tree, so that the blessing of Abraham may come upon me, Jason Alvarez (put your name there), through Jesus Christ, that I might receive the promise of the Spirit through faith. Galatians 3:13-14

   Therefore I boldly confess, that Abraham's blessings are my portion. Today I boldly confess, I'm blessed coming in and I'm blessed going out, I'm blessed in the city and I'm blessed in the field, whatsoever I set my hands too, Father I thank You that You cause it to flourish, prosper, and succeed at my hands. I praise You, Father, that when my enemies rise up against me, they are smitten before my face. They come against me one way, but flee from before me seven different ways [in total defeat].

   Today I praise You, Father, for making me the head and not the tail, for putting me above only and never beneath, for causing me to ride upon the high places of the earth, and for keeping me as the apple of Your eye, safe and sound from harm, dangers, accidents, and freakish things and vandalism in Jesus's name. Father, today I boldly confess that because Abraham's blessings are mine, You command the blessing upon me in my store houses. [So that my bank accounts overflow.] I praise you Father, that You command the blessing upon me in all that I set my hands to [so that everything I do or involve myself in flourishes, prospers. and succeeds]. I boldly confess, I now possess the golden touch!

I praise You, Father, that You command the blessing upon me in the good land You have given me in Jesus name. [In Deuteronomy 8, God said, if you obey me, I'll bless you with homes you didn't build and vineyards you didn't plant.]

10. Here is a power prayer to stop Satan at the onset:
Satan, it is written: God frustrates and disappoints your devices so that your hands cannot perform their enterprises against me. I say you meet with darkness in the daytime and you grope in the noonday as in the nighttime and all your plans and all of your strategies are of no effect to work against me, my family, or my ministry in Jesus' mighty name.

11. Finally, here is a prayer in which Kind David acknowledged God's greatness, *and so should we:*
"Thine, O Lord, is the Greatness, and the Power, and the Glory, and the Victory, and the Majesty: for all that is in the heavens and in the earth is thine; For thine is the Kingdom, O Lord, and thou art Exalted as head above all. Both riches and honour come of thee, and thou reignest over all; and in thine hand is power and might; and in thine hand it is to make great, and to give strength unto all". (1 Chronicles 29:11-12) So today I praise you for your Awesomeness and Greatness in Jesus' name, amen!

Chapter 3

The Third
M—Moods

In the Gospel of John 14:27, Jesus said, "My Peace I leave with you; my [own] peace I now give and bequeath to you. So let not your hearts be troubled, neither let them be afraid." The Greek reads, Stop allowing yourselves to be "agitated and disturbed." I say amen!

A mood is defined as a temporary state of mind or feeling. To me, a mood is a temporary mind shift. This could take place upon hearing something said or by simply seeing a specific person or thing, and bam! Immediately, our psyche reacts with a temporary mind shift, or what I call *moods*. The change can be positive or negative, good or bad, uplifting or depressing. I have discovered that it mainly depends on our filtering system and mind-set as it relates to how we perceive situations.

I realize that some mood changes come as a result of chemical events in the physical body. And it is also clear to me that there is an interchange between the mental/emotional and our physical bodies, such that things that occur in the physical body can affect moods, and vice versa. But let's focus on moods as relates to our ability to control them, because this is a truth that we all need to be clear on.

For example, if you're not used to harnessing your thoughts or exercising self-control when situations present themselves, your mood swings will probably be more frequent and last a lot longer than you might desire. On the other hand, if you learn to deliberately exercise authority over what you will and will not think about and entertain, and if you choose the feelings that you will and will not react to, then your mood swings will probably not be as frequent or severe. And when they do occur, they will not last as long. Now, I know that this teaching might seem strange, but don't just take my word for it; let's look into the Bible and see what it has to say about it.

In Proverbs 25:28, Solomon, the wisest man to ever live, wrote, "He that Hath No Rule over his own spirit is like a city that is Broken Down, and Without Walls." This simply says that if you don't exercise control over your own life—though in this case, I'm talking about your thought life—you're like a city without walls. [In other words, you are totally Defenseless Against the Attacks of the enemy.] Now listen to this same scripture in the Message Bible translation: "A person Without Self-Control is like a house with its doors and windows knocked out." Wow! Now, can you see what I'm talking about? Bottom line is, you can't allow your moods to control you; rather, you must learn to control them, or else you will become a basket case.

The truth is, the attitude you have while you are in the wilderness will determine how long you will be there. Joyce Meyer said, "If you complain, you will remain, but if you praise, you will be raised." It's totally up to you!

Speaking of moods, something happened to me yesterday that put me in a very depressed mood for a lot longer than I'm accustomed.

Everything was going great. I had just come out of the recording studio, where I was working on my new album, and was happy as can be. Suddenly, one of my secretaries walked into my office and said, "Pastor, Oliver—Jean's husband—just died!"

I said, "What? What did you just say?" She repeated it. Talk about a mind shift! Immediately, I went from being on the mountaintop to plunging into a deep valley … just like that! Have you ever been there? Well, her news really, really rocked me, and I must admit, I went totally numb.

Even an hour later, I just couldn't seem to shake it, no matter how hard I tried. Finally, about two hours later, I was having dinner with my wife, and I guess it must have been obvious to her, because she kept asking me, "J, are you all right? J, what's the matter?" So I finally told her. And when I did that, she kindly expressed her sympathy and went on to diligently pray for me, which I greatly appreciated.

It wasn't until a couple hours later, and after much effort, that I was able to finally push that depressed mood off of me and go on to enjoy the rest of the night. No matter how strong we think we are, certain news, events, and other encounters generally play a large role in the kinds of moods we all experience. I'm saying this because the next day, when I walked into my office, one of my workers came up to me and said, "Pastor, after having heard the news about Oliver yesterday, I got so depressed that I could hardly sleep at all. Sorry, this is why I'm so tired today." Immediately I thought, *Man, had I not fought back and pushed this thing off of me when I did, I'm sure Oliver's news would have ruined not just my dinner, but also my entire night, just like it did his.* Right then, I heard the Lord say, "Son, learn from this, because life is too precious and too short for you to allow yourself to be moody and upset all the time! Remember, you are free!"

This is why I am convinced that where the mind goes, the emotions, and ultimately the man follows. And unless we rise up and learn to take control over our thought life and emotions, they will ultimately take control of us.

That is why I frequently ask myself these questions:

1. Is this news or situation worth getting depressed over or losing my peace over?
2. Or what good will it do me to lose sleep over something that is totally out of my reach and control?

3. Or why should I allow myself to get overwhelmed with something that I can't do anything about?
4. Or, "J, why don't you just cast this care over on God and move on with your life?"

Because the truth is that nothing, absolutely nothing, is worth you and me losing our peace and victory over. And isn't this is exactly what Jesus instructed us in John 14:27?

The message is clear, especially when you read it from the Amplified version of the Bible, in which it is written that Jesus said, "Peace I leave with you; My [own] peace I now give and bequeath to you. Not as the world gives do I give to you my peace. Do not let your hearts be troubled, neither let them be afraid."

This peace is our inheritance because Jesus has bequeathed or given His peace to us. However, it is totally up to us to protect it, hold on to it, and not let anyone or anything snatch it away. Why? Because the enemy knows that if he can rob your peace, He will take your victory and steal your joy!

Next, Jesus said, "Stop allowing yourselves to be agitated and disturbed."

So, no matter what is going on in our lives, the Lord totally expects us to take a strong stand against the enemy and not to *allow ourselves* to be agitated and disturbed. This tells me that we are in charge. We are in control. But if you don't learn to stand up to the devil and use the authority Jesus Christ has given you in His name, then the enemy will have you walking on pins and needles, always agitated, always disturbed and freaked out over one thing or another. But that's not all, beause Jesus goes deeper yet and says, "Do not permit yourselves to be fearful, intimidated, cowardly, and unsettled." In other words, whatever we permit is what He will permit. This is also what I believe the Lord meant when he said, "Whatsoever you shall bind on earth, shall be bound in heaven and whatsoever you shall loose on earth, shall be loosed in heaven." The Good News Testament puts it this way: "And so I tell all of you: what you prohibit on earth will be prohibited in heaven, and what you permit on earth will be permitted in heaven." My goodness, man, can you see it? Now, *do it!*

A Vision

This is why I'll never forget the vision that Kenneth Hagin once had. He said that Jesus appeared to him and began speaking to him about some very important things, when all of a sudden, a demon came out of nowhere, stepped in between the Lord and him, and began yelling at the top of his voice. Well, it was so loud that Brother Hagin could no longer hear Jesus speaking. Hagin said,

> I was so shocked by the fact that this demon was able to do this, and even more shocked by the fact that Jesus was doing nothing about it, he said, I became more and more frustrated, until I just couldn't take it anymore. Suddenly, I started yelling and rebuking the demon at the top of my lungs, commanding him, "You foul spirit, I command you in the name of Jesus Christ of Nazareth to get out of the way right now, and come back no more, in Jesus's name!" And to my utter amazement, the demon looked at me with big sad eyes and said, "Okay, okay, I'll go if you say so," and with that he fled the house as one in terror, just like the Bible says. I couldn't believe it. So with that, I asked the Lord, "Lord, why didn't you do something about that demon? Why did you allow him to interfere and get in between us like that?" The Lord then rocked my theology by saying, "Son, if you hadn't done something about it, I couldn't have."

So I asked him, "Why? You are Almighty God. You are the Resurrected Savior. You are the King of Kings. Why couldn't you have done something about it?" He said to me, "Because I have given you, the Church, the authority to cast out demons in my name and in my place. So if you hadn't done it, I could not have done it for you."

Wow! Wow! Wow! Now can you see it? From this I learned that the devil can only go as far as we let him. Why? Because you're in control!

Mood and Atmosphere Go Hand in Hand

Now, here's another thing I have discovered concerning moods: Mood and atmosphere go hand in hand. Oh yes, I'm convinced that the atmosphere you swim in and create around you will greatly affect your moods. For example, I remember when my secretary's office, which was the only way into mine, was very unattractive and definitely not conducive to a healthy or creative atmosphere. I hated having to go through there. So one day, I decided I would have it remodeled. And man, the difference was like night and day! So much so that now, when I step into that office, I am lifted, happy to be there, and many times I am inspired.

I once heard someone say that the atmosphere you create determines what lives or dies in you. Man, do I agree! Is it any wonder that heaven is such an amazing place? Think about it. The Almighty doesn't sit on a wooden bench to rule the universe from. No, He sits on a glorious throne! He doesn't walk on streets made of dirt, but on streets paved with gold. The walls in heaven are not made out of Sheetrock, but precious jewels and costly stones. Is it any wonder then why heaven's atmosphere is completely infused and wonderfully decorated with awe-inspiring and beautiful things? Aren't you glad Jesus didn't say, "In my Father's house are many ghetto shacks, and I'm going there to build a special one just for you." No, a million times no! Instead, He enthusiastically informed His disciples and us, "In my Father's house are many mansions and one of them has your name on it." So yes, my friend, atmosphere matters!

I have come to see that the right atmosphere is vital to our experiences and existence. I strongly believe it is one of the main vehicles God uses to take us to the land of divine inspiration and the world of supernatural creativity.

Take church for example. Why do you think we have praise and worship in a service? The answer is simple: to create an atmosphere conducive for God to manifest Himself and do signs and wonders.

I want to be very careful how I say this, but I believe music puts God in a good mood. And don't you want to put Him in a good mood? I'm sure the answer is "yes and amen!"

In Psalm 22:3, we see how important it is for us to create the right atmosphere for God Almighty to set up His throne in our midst and manifest His glory. "But You are holy, O You who dwell in [the holy place where] the praises of Israel are offered."

Think about the workplace. I believe that before the breath of inspiration can begin to flow and birth the most creative and productive person one could ever be, the proper atmosphere should be created, even in the work environment.

How about relationships? Let's look at it from a negative side. What kind of atmosphere do you think strife and divisions create? They create an uneasy and tense atmosphere that sometimes feels like you can literally cut it with a knife.

I have discovered that this is the kind of atmosphere in which bad things grow and good things die. I call it "the birthing place for demonic activity."

The mood created there is hostile, hopeless, and depressing, often creating the kind of atmosphere that is conducive for evil spirits to manifest themselves and make life a living hell. Trust me: been there, done that! And let me add, *overcome that!* For example,

I remember a time, many years ago, when I would wake up in an excellent mood, only to find myself, minutes later, walking into a war zone known as my kitchen.

There, among other places, the atmosphere at times would become so charged with strife that in just a few moments, my wife and I would find ourselves in a stone-throwing contest and tearing each other up like wild animals with destructive and malicious words. Paul speaks to us about that very situation, writing, "If you continue hurting each other and tearing each other apart, be careful, or you will completely destroy each other" (Gal. 5:15). Isn't that the truth?

Well, needless to say, for the rest of the day after these bouts, I struggled greatly just to keep my head above water. Honestly, it felt as if I had a dark cloud constantly hanging over my head and an invisible hand around my neck trying to suffocate me. Thank God those days are gone forever, and now my wife and I are experiencing "heaven on earth." But those days were not easy! (I'll be sharing more about this when we get to the M&M's of marriage.) Now here is the good news: If you dare put into practice what I'm sharing with you in this book, I believe that, in time, you too will experience the same results, if not better, for God is no respecter of persons.

Let me say it again, because this is a truth that we all need to be clear on and have under our belt: If you're not used to harnessing your thoughts or exercising self-control when situations present themselves, your mood swings will probably be more frequent and last a lot longer than you desire. On the other hand, if you learn to deliberately exercise authority over what you will and will not think about and entertain, and if you choose the feelings that you will and will not react to, then your mood swings will probably not be as frequent or severe. And when they do occur, they will not last as long. Remember, you are in control, and not your feelings.

Right now, I prophesy that change is coming your way. Fear not; your best is yet ahead!

Chapter 4

The Fourth M—Motives

For we must all appear and be revealed as we are before the judgment seat of Christ, so that each one may receive [his pay] according to what he has done in the body, whether good or evil [considering what his purpose and motive have been, and what he has achieved, been busy with, and given himself and his attention to accomplishing].

—2 Corinthians 5:10 (AMP)

Here's my definition of *motives*: Why you do what you do!

The reason I feel impelled to write a small chapter on the subject of motives is because, over the course of the years, mine have not always been right. As a result, I have wasted a lot of precious time settling for a few crumbs or a few moments of vain glory (the praises and approval of men), when all the while, I could have had the whole loaf and the praises of the Father.

I have learned that in the sight of God, it is not so much *what you do* that counts as much as *why you do what you do*. In other words, your motives and not your actions are mainly what God is looking at and judging. For it is written, "man looks on the outward

Chapter 5

The Fifth
M—Money

> And Isaac sowed in that land, and reaped in the same year a hundredfold [or 100 times as much]; and the Lord blessed him. And the man began to prosper and continued prospering until he became very prosperous.
>
> —Genesis 26:12

Let me begin this chapter by misquoting a scripture, because that is what so many people do. They'll say, "the Bible says, 'Money is the root of all evil'!" Wrong! That's not what the scripture teaches. But what the Bible does teach is, "the love of money [not money, but the *love of* money] is the root of all evil" (1 Tim. 6:10).

Would you believe it if I told you that the lack of money is often more devastating than the love of money?

Are you aware that more marriages will end in divorce this year for the lack of money, than for the love of money?

Are you aware that more churches will close their doors this year for the lack of money than for the love of money?

Are you aware that more children will starve to death this year for the lack of money than for the love of money?

When the Lord showed me this, I immediately saw that money in and of itself is not evil. It's just a matter of who's handling it. I also learned that money makes a terrible God but a good servant. For example, if you give money to a good man, he will most likely wind up doing something good with it. On the other hand, if you give money to a drug dealer, he will most likely wind up doing something evil with it. Again, it's a matter of who is handling the money. However, in and of itself, money has no mind of its own.

Let me tell you something else I learned firsthand about money: Money can't buy you love, like the song says, or friendship or loyalty or even happiness, and sure enough, it can't ever buy you your salvation. I know lots of people who have plenty of money but who are not very happy.

On the other hand, I am a witness that money can be a great blessing. If handled correctly, it can meet lots and lots of needs and do lots and lots of good.

I've also discovered that money will never be able to fuel or fully satisfy the emptiness in your heart, no matter how much money you have. Only Jesus and healthy relationships can. This is why I tell everyone I meet that I am rich, and the reason I'm rich is not only because I have plenty of money, but mainly because of the amazing relationships I have and enjoy all around the world and because I know that I know I'm saved.

A Bit of My Story

Allow me to share a little bit of my story. Did you know that there was a time when I was very famous? Oh yes, in case you didn't know, mine was the golden voice on the hit song "Shame, Shame, Shame" in the early seventies, which topped the Billboard charts both here and abroad and sold millions of records. So as a result, during that period of my life, money, drugs, women, and fame were all at my beck and call.

And yet with all of this, my heart had never been so empty, and I had never felt so alone. Would you believe it if I told you that I even felt this emptiness in the midst of very large crowds? And by large crowds, I'm talking about tens of thousands of adoring fans. That's when I discovered that loneliness really had nothing to do with others and everything to do with myself. The truth is that, although I was famous and doing financially well, I was a pretty miserable dude. But it wasn't until we went on our European tour that things really spiraled out of control. I remember sitting on the floor of a penthouse in a London hotel with a fellow songwriter named Scott English, who back then had written many great hit songs, including one of my all-time favorites, "Under the Boardwalk." Well, his song "Brandy" had climbed to number two on the charts (it would later be recorded by Barry Manilow as "Mandy") while my song, "Shame, Shame, Shame," had claimed the number-one spot. I can still remember sitting on the floor with him, passing a marijuana joint back and forth, when suddenly he asked me a question that would *change my life forever*: "Man, *is this all there is to life?*" he asked. Wow! That question made me start thinking. Here we were—I had the number-one hit record in London, and Scott had the number two—but deep down inside both of us, we knew something was missing.

We knew there was more to life. We just didn't know what it was.

In that very moment, I realized that there was a big, big hole in my heart, that nothing I had accomplished or experienced up to that point could satisfy or fill—not money, not fame, not even women or drugs. Nothing. Man, I'm telling you, the spirit of despair immediately began to dog my heels, and I found myself plunging into a deep state of depression and entertaining relentless thoughts of suicide. Those thoughts were coming at me faster than machine-gun bullets. I'll never forget that day as long as I live, because that was the day I began to think about taking my own life. I even wrote a suicide letter, which I still have.

By the next morning, I was beginning to seriously contemplate jumping out of a huge window in the penthouse and just end it all.

But just as I was ready to take the plunge, it suddenly hit me: "Man, that's a long, long way down, and if I jump out of this window, and with my luck just get all crippled up and don't die, then my life will be an even bigger mess." So I decided to wait until I got back to America, and then I would kill myself, but not in such a violent way.

All I can say is thank God for His supernatural intervention, because not long after that, I met my Savior Jesus Christ, and in an instant, my long-time search came to an end, and I was born again.

So yes, my friend, I know firsthand that money can buy you lots and lots of nice things, and meet lots and lots of needs, because I had all of that and more, but I found out that money alone cannot fuel nor ever come near to satisfying the deep longings of your heart. Only Jesus and healthy relationships can.

Know This: Lack of Knowledge Will Cost You!

I can remember many times, even after I became a Christian, when my family and I fasted, not because we wanted to, but because we had no money for food. Now that's what I call living from hand to mouth! I still recall the night when a young mother and her little baby showed up at our house asking us to help her buy milk and diapers for her baby. You would not believe it, but we were so broke that, after searching the whole house, all we were able to come up with was a little more than a dollar. Is it any wonder even poor folk called us poor?

So we gave her what little money we came up with and fervently prayed for her and the baby. Unfortunately, that was the best we could do that night. Needless to say, from that night on, I would never look at money the same. That's when it dawned on me that if we were going to help people and fulfill the call that was on our life and our ministry, we would need money—lots of it, because we had big dreams. Yet, in spite of all our continued financial struggles, we went on serving God to the best of our abilities, believing that somehow he would make a way for us, and thank God He did.

Seed Power

Then one glorious night, I heard the great T.L. Osborn teach on the subject of "seed power"! Man, I had never heard anything like that before. I tell you, that was definitely a benchmark moment in my life. Since then, I've learned much about the principle of sowing and reaping, what T.L. Osborn calls "seed power." So allow me to share with you some of those truths and some of the amazing testimonies I have experienced.

To begin with, I never knew I could sow my very own money as seed in the same way a farmer puts his seeds into the ground for growth of a future harvest. You might say, "Yes, I know all that." Well I didn't know it, and as a result, the devil had me living from hand to mouth, or as Hosea 4:6 teaches, I was being destroyed for lack of knowledge.

So I diligently began searching the scriptures as the Bereans did to see if those things were so. And to my delight, I discovered what many theologians call the law of Genesis, which says that everything reproduces after its own kind. For example, dogs reproduce dogs, cats reproduce cats, apples reproduce apples, and tomatoes reproduce tomatoes. This truth was affirmed to me with Paul's teaching in Galatians 6:7, which says, "Be not deceived; God is not mocked: for whatsoever a man soweth, that shall he also reap."

These scriptures taught me that if I wanted a harvest of tomatoes. I needed to sow tomato seeds. If I wanted a harvest of love, I should then sow seeds of love. It became very clear to me that if I wanted a harvest of money, I needed to sow some money. Why? Because the law of all laws teaches us that everything reproduces after its own kind.

Honestly, that teaching changed everything. I remember my wife and me getting so turned on to this principle that when we didn't have any money to sow, we just started pulling pictures off the walls of our home and sowing them. Literally, we sowed anything and everything that we could get our hands on.

Now this is the truth: Within a few months, God began performing such financial miracles in our lives that, many times, as David of old wrote in Psalm 126:1, we thought we were *dreaming*. Ever since we received this simple revelation and began applying it, we've been on a roll, and thank God, it hasn't stopped yet!

Since then, I have learned two more amazing truths about this area of money and giving that I would love to share with you. I truly believe they will be as life-changing for you as they have been for me.

1. Proportion

I discovered that you will always reap in proportion to what you sow. I don't really know if this can be said any more simply, but to me, this is plain common sense. But don't just take my word for it; let's see what the Bible has to say about it.

> Listen to Paul:

> But this I say, he which soweth nothing shall reap *nothing!* "He that soweth sparingly (or stingily) shall reap also sparingly [or stingily] and he which soweth bountifully (or abundantly) shall reap also bountifully (or abundantly) every man according as he purposeth in his heart, so let him give; not grudgingly, or of necessity: for God loveth a cheerful giver. Or A Giver, whose Heart is in his/her Giving".
> 2 Cor. 9:6

Then in Luke 6:38 (AMP), Jesus himself reinforced this amazing principle. Listen to it!

> "Give, and [gifts] will be given to you; good measure, pressed down, shaken together, and running over, will they pour into [the pouch formed by] the bosom [of your robe and used as a bag]. For with

the *measure you deal out [or with the measure you use when you confer benefits on others] it will be measured back to you."*

In other words, the law of sowing and reaping says that the size of your harvest does not depend on God, *but on you.* For you will always REAP in proportion to what you have sown.

For example, sow nothing—reap nothing! Sow little—reap little! Sow much—reap much!

2. Attitude and God's Response

This is important: The attitude with which you give will determine God's response.

The Amplified Bible says it this way:

> For God loves (He takes pleasure in, prizes above other things, and is unwilling to abandon or to do without) a cheerful (joyous, "prompt to do it") giver (whose heart is in his/her giving).[Or God gets blessed, by those who give with a smile.] 2 Corinthians 9-7 AMPC

Have you ever met anyone like that? I did. It happened for me while I was on a mission trip to Africa. He was a Christian brother who, in my estimation, was extremely critical of others and very hard to get along with. (But little did I know that he was being mightily used by God.) So in my immaturity, I asked the Lord, "Why are You keeping this guy around, Lord? Can't you see that nobody likes him?" The Lord responded, "Son, this man is one of my greatest givers. And haven't you heard, I am unwilling to abandon (or to do without) a cheerful (joyous, "prompt to do it") giver [whose heart is in his giving]? And for your information, this is one of those men.

"Moreover, I'll have you know that, with great joy, he has been supporting this entire African mission work, which for years has been used to raise up many great leaders throughout the entire continent of Africa and around the world. So leave him alone and mind your own business."

Man, I quickly repented and never messed with that guy again.

Right then and there, I saw God's attitude toward a giver. But after all, who's a greater giver than our heavenly Father? The answer is, no one!

3. Sowing in Your Famine!

Lastly here, I want to talk to you about the importance of sowing when your back is up against the wall. This is what the Bible calls "sowing in a time of famine." I recall Dr. Norvel Hayes once saying, when I was young in the Lord, "If you never want to go broke, make sure you sow your last twenty dollars." In other words, don't ever eat your last seed; sow it! And isn't this exactly what Genesis 26:12 teaches us? "Then (in time of famine) Isaac sowed in that land, and received in the same year an hundredfold [or a hundred times as much]: and the Lord blessed him."

Have you ever been in a famine? The closest I've ever come to one was in Cuba, It was right after Fidel Castro had taken over. And although it was not really as much a famine as it was a drastic rationing of food and a time of unusual lack, for me, that was famine.

However, I have seen stories of real famine on television, and I have also read extensively about them. For example, I once read that the world's deadliest famine killed an estimated 30 million people in China. The famine was caused by a drought, which was followed by crop failure, which was then followed by starvation, disease, and cannibalism.

Did you say *cannibalism*?

Yes, you heard right: even cannibalism.

Now, if you are a student of the Bible, you are well aware that there were times when this very condition occurred in Bible days. Various passages describe the same kind of devastation that we have seen in modern times.

I bring all this up in order to arouse your imagination as to what was happening with Isaac in the passage we just read. You see, Isaac was living in Gerar, with the Philistines. This territory would eventually be the dwelling place of his children in generations to come. But while he was there, a real famine took place, just like one of the famines I described earlier. Yet, in the midst of drought, starvation, disease and even cannibalism, something powerful must have happened to him.

I personally believe that somehow, in his mind's eye or memory bank, he pressed the Replay button and began to think about his miraculous birth. I'm sure he thought of his amazing experience with Abraham, his father, on Mount Moriah, where the angel of the Lord appeared to Abraham—right when Abraham was ready to plunge the knife into Isaac's heart—and said, "Abraham! Abraham! Lay not thine hand upon the lad, neither do thou any thing unto him: for now I know that you Love Me, seeing thou hast not withheld thy son, thine only son from me." (Genesis 22:12) Then, I believe, Isaac began playing over and over again in his heart and mind the prophecies that God Almighty had spoken over him, just like he's spoken over you, and *bam!* Just like a bolt of lightning, faith struck him—the God kind of faith, faith that will *not be denied,* the kind of faith that moves the hand that moves the world. It struck him from the top of his head to the soles of his feet, and suddenly, he began boldly declaring, "I will live and not die and declare the works of the Lord. With long life He will satisfy me and show me His salvation." And because faith is an action, Isaac, although fatigued as he was from the famine, somehow drew strength from the Mighty One of Israel, picked up his shovel, began breaking up the fallow ground with it and sowing his seeds of faith. Remember, he did this dead smack in the middle of a real famine. This act of faith got all of heaven's attention, including God's?

I believe that it was right then and there that Isaac's faith moved the hand that moves the world, and all at once, God dispatched his angels to work on Isaac's behalf. And the Bible says, "Isaac Received (or Reaped) in the same year One hundred fold [or a Hundred Times More than He Sowed], and the Lord Blessed Him."(Gen. 26:12) I would say so! Now listen to what the Bible says next: "And the man waxed great, and went forward, and grew until he became very great: "For he had possession of flocks, and possession of herds, and great store of servants: and the Philistines envied him." Gen. 26:13-14

Testimonials of God's Faithfulness

Let me share with you just a few personal testimonies of the miracles that God has performed for me as I have learned these truths and walked out these principles.

Vinnie with Food

Do you remember me telling you that we often fasted, not because we wanted to, but because we had no money for food? Well, here's the amazing thing: Not long after we started sowing and believing God would perform miracles, little by little, things began to change.

I remember the night it all started. It was as if someone had suddenly opened a heavenly faucet, and supernatural blessings began flowing out and overtaking us.

The miracles began when a young man, Vinnie, surprised us by coming to our house and started blessing us with boxes and boxes of all kinds of meats and pasta and vegetables and fruits. Man, I couldn't believe it! And suddenly, for the first time in a very long time, our refrigerator was full, and so were our bellies. These amazing miracles of divine provision continued for close to a year. But it was only the beginning!

A Widow in Mexico

I remember being on a missions trip to Mexico when, out of nowhere, a beautiful lady came up to me and said, "Here, Jason, I've been saving my tithes for a while and the Lord told me to give them to you." It was a little pouch filled with hundred-dollar bills!

That little pouch had more money in it than I had made for the entire year.

My First Dream House

I recall buying my first dream house. I had been praying, fasting on and off, sowing financial seeds, and confessing the Word of God for almost three years. My confession was, "I believe, I receive a dream house for a supernatural price in Jesus's name, and I shall have it."

Long story short, I found the dream house in an exclusive area that was selling for $600,000. I can still remember when I first began negotiating with the owner of the house. I remember saying to him, "I will be happy to give you $225,000 for the house."

I'll never forget what he said: "Are you crazy? This is a brand-new house and the least I'll take is $550,000!"

So I came back to him with "I'll give you $227,500."

He responded, "I don't think you're hearing me." He said, "The best I can do is $450,000."

I said, "Okay, I'll give you $230,000."

He looked at me and said, "Man, I can't believe you! Look, the best I can do is 350. And that's my best price." Well, we went back and forth, until he finally said, "This is my last price. It is a gentleman's price. I'll give it to you for $245,000."

I responded, "Well I'm a gentleman; I'll take it." That's how I got my first dream house for a supernatural price—which house, by the way, I later sold to a doctor for close to a million!

This is why I always say it pays to Honor God and sow financial seeds for miracles!

The Grand Piano

Sometime after we moved into our house, a friend said to me, "Pastor, that house needs a baby grand piano!" I thought to myself, *He's right*, but I didn't have any money. So when I picked up my children from school that day, I told them that, before we went home, we needed to stop at the baby grand piano dealer.

They asked me, "Are you going to buy a piano today, Daddy?"

I answered, "No, I'm going to lay hands on one and believe God will perform a miracle for us."

It just so happened that later that night, I was going to Albany, New York, to minister. While I was at the church preaching, I saw not a baby grand, but a full-length, brand-new Yamaha grand piano sitting in the sanctuary. Wouldn't you know it? It had never been played before. (Nothing but God!) All I remember is that I ran up to that piano and said to the audience, "Today, I laid my hands on a piano just like this and claimed it in Jesus's name."

Suddenly, a woman from the audience jumped up and enthusiastically shouted, "Pastor Jason! That's my piano, and God just told me to give it to you!"

Ha-ha-ha! I still have it, and I have written many wonderful songs on that piano that have touched the lives of multitudes of people around the world. To God be all the glory!

A 1929 Mercedes

One day, I walked into a businessman's house on Staten Island. We were having a conversation, when out of the clear blue, this man said to me, "Young man, I believe God is telling me to give you one of my cars."

I responded, "I don't doubt it!"

It was a 1929 Mercedes Benz with forty-eight original miles on it!

It became the talk of the entire community where I bought my first dream house.

Madison Square Garden Miracle

I could go on and on with these testimonies, but I'll share one last miracle with you.

It was a Wednesday night after our service, when a man named George Seiber walked into the vestibule of the church I was renting at the time and asked for Jason Alvarez.

I told him, "I am Jason."

He said to me, "I heard you sing and lead worship."

I responded that I did. Then to my delight, he said, "I am hosting a meeting at Madison Square Garden in New York City this Friday night, and I would like for you to do the music for us." Then he asked me, "How much would you charge?" My answer was, "I don't charge for the Gospel. But if God gives me the green light, I will be glad to do it for free." Little did I know that this man was very rich. Now remember, by this time, we had been sowing what little money we had according to the teaching we had heard by T. L. Osborn on seed power. Only this time, I wasn't just going to be sowing my money; I was going to be sowing my time and my talent as well, which I had no problem doing.

So I led the worship service at Madison Square Garden that Friday night, and it was a huge success, because many people were saved and greatly blessed. Now here's the most amazing thing about that whole experience: After the Madison Square Garden event, my friendship with that wealthy man continued. Little did I know that God would mightily use this man to change the course of my life. I am giving you the short version, but in case you're interested, the rest of this miracle story, and many others like it, will be included in my new book, *From Shame to Glory*, being released soon.

Purchasing a Church

About four months later, the kind of church building you only dream of became available for the kind of money most people never have. When my rich friend heard about the church becoming available, he asked me to take him to see it. So I did. Then, a couple days later, I received a call from him: "J, my wife and I have been praying about this church building, and we believe God wants you to have it, because from there, God is going to use you and your ministry to touch the world. J, you've got to get this building."

So I responded, "I know, George. But I don't have the money." Well, we negotiated back and forth for the purchase of the church for months, until finally I stepped out in faith and struck a deal to buy the building. Mind you, I didn't have a dime, but I had faith that God would somehow perform a miracle. And so the big day came when we were supposed to close on the deal. Honestly, I had no idea where the money was going to come from, but I knew deep down in my knower that God was somehow going to come through for me.

We had two hours left to come up with the money, when suddenly I received a phone call from Mr. Seiber, who said, "J, please wait for me. My plane just landed, and I will be at your house in thirty minutes." When he showed up in my house, the first thing he said was, "J's, God told my wife and me that you have to buy this church!"

I said, "George, I know it, but I don't have any money." So he began to pace back and forth and continued telling me the same thing over and over again. And like a broken record, I kept saying the same thing to him. "I know George, but I don't have any money." (I can still see him now!)

Finally, after about twenty minutes, he stopped, turned around, and asked me. "J, how much money do you need?" So I told him. He paused for a moment; then he simply put his hand in his jacket pocket, pulled out a small checkbook, wrote a check with a lot of zeros on it, and handed it to me. With that he said, "J, I told you, God said to me and my wife, you need to buy that church. Now go and get it!" All I can say is, God performed a great miracle for us that day!

And that miracle saga continues, because from the time we opened our doors, The Love of Jesus Family Church has been a womb of blessings for many people here and around the world. Literally hundreds of ministries have been birthed and raised up there and are presently serving God around the world, and many more are even now in the birthing process and in training as I write this book. The truth is, everything George and his wife prophesied would happen has happened and is still coming to pass. To God be all the glory!

Remember, all the flowers of all your tomorrows, are in the seeds you plant today!

Chapter 6

The Sixth M— Ministry

For I am now ready to be offered, and the time of my departure is at hand. I have fought a good fight, I have finished my course, I have kept the faith: Henceforth there is laid up for me a crown of righteousness, which the Lord, the righteous judge, shall give me at that day: and not to me only, but unto all them also that love his appearing.

—2 Timothy 4:6–8

I can clearly remember the day God supernaturally allowed me to take a peep into the future. At that time, we lived in an old house in Bloomfield, New Jersey.

I had just gotten home from church early that afternoon, while my wife had gone ahead of me to a Youth Retreat in Hope, New Jersey, to assist as a youth counselor for the next six days.

I decided to eat lunch alone on my screened-in back porch, which overlooked my backyard, and relax there awhile, when suddenly I had a vision! In it, I saw a man running back and forth on a platform. This guy was preaching like a house on fire. I thought, "Who is this guy?" Meanwhile, he kept preaching and running from one end of the platform to the other. When all of a sudden, the man stopped, turned around, and looked straight at me. And to my total amazement, when I saw his face, it was I!

I couldn't believe it. I was in shock. Then I heard the voice of the Lord clearly say to me:

> Rise, and stand upon thy feet, for I have appeared unto thee for this purpose, to make thee a minister and a witness both of these things which thou hast seen, and of those things in the which I will appear unto thee; delivering thee from the people, and from the gentiles, unto whom now I send thee, to open their eyes, and to turn them from darkness to light and from the power of Satan unto God, that they may receive forgiveness of sins and an inheritance among them which are sanctified by faith that is in me.

When the vision was over, I must admit it left me scratching my head and wondering; what in the world just happened? I had never experienced anything like this before. So I just committed it to God and went on to finish my lunch. Later that afternoon, I drove up to the youth camp where my wife was, to see if there was anything I could do to help. When I arrived there, I didn't say a word to anyone about the vision I had experienced. I simply saw my wife for a brief moment, said hello to her and immediately went looking for the man in charge, as I had heard they were short-handed. When I found him and made myself available to him, he seemed relieved. He then quickly asked me, "Can you cook hot dogs and hamburgers?"

I replied, "Is the pope Catholic? Of course I can."

He then asked, "Can you also take care of putting away all the garbage cans tonight?"

I replied, "Sure! I'm here to do whatever you need!"

Finally, I went to bed that night laughing to myself, thinking the vision I had was probably the result of the pepperoni pizza I ate for lunch, or maybe it was just simply a crazy figment of my imagination. So I shrugged it off and eventually went to sleep.

But early the next morning at breakfast, the man in charge of the youth camp came to me and asked, "Can you preach this morning?"

I answered, "Preach?"

He said, "Yeah, preach! I believe you have a word for the young people this morning."

Man, I couldn't believe it. Me preach? Then I remembered the vision. So I preached that morning on the Book of Jonah. Just don't ask me what the content was, because all I remember was me running back and forth from one end of the platform to the other, just as I saw myself in the vision. So there it is: funny, but that was my introduction into the ministry.

Called to Pastoral Ministry

Let me tell you the story of what I believe was my official call to the pastoral ministry. It was a Friday night, and we were in a service in New York City, where my wife was ministering. I remember the service had ended and a few people were hanging around fellowshipping. Suddenly, I heard the Lord ask me, "J, do you love Me?"

I said, "Yes Lord, I love You."

He said, "Feed My sheep." Again He asked me, "J, do you love Me?"

So I answered, "Yes, Lord, You know that I love You."

He said, "Feed My sheep."

By that point, I was embarrassed because I had started weeping in front of all these people. Yet they didn't really know what was going on, because this conversation was taking place in my heart, inside me. Then, He asked me the third time, "J, do you love Me?"

This time, while weeping, I answered with my voice, "Yes, Lord, You know that I love You!"

Then He asked me, "Will you feed My lambs?"

And I responded, "Yes, Lord, I will feed Your lambs!" I'm telling you man, I will never ever forget that experience.

And I know this is how He called Peter, but nevertheless, it is also how He called me. Looking back, I can clearly see that this was the night He officially called me to pastor His precious people. And although I didn't start pastoring until many years later, I believe that was the night God's holy anointing oil was supernaturally poured on my head, just as in the days of old, when the prophet Samuel poured the holy oil upon David's head, signifying God's calling and separation.

Little did I know that I had been enlisted into the school of the Holy Spirit, better known as God's boot camp. Let me tell you, this school is not for the weak in heart or for quitters. I would dare say what the United States Navy Seals have to endure in order to become a part of those Special Forces is no different from what we have to go through in the Spirit in order to qualify for ministry.

Let me offer you an example: the test of patience. Man, I can't begin to count the times when impatience got the best of me. And I'm sure I'm not in this one by myself. Just ask Abraham! Now think about it: Who in the world wants to take that test? Not me! However, I have learned that if you want to survive and succeed in ministry, you must not only take these tests, but you must also pass them.

For example, not long ago, I took on the challenge of designing and building a house to sell later for a profit. It became one of the greatest challenges in my life. The process was grueling, to say the least. After a while, I felt like just giving up. Then one day, when things seemed to be going from bad to worse, God in his mercy whispered in my ear. "J, it is important that during this season in your life, you learn the secret of making patience your friend." Wow, I had never heard that before. But then I remembered Hebrews 6:11–15: "And we desire that every one of you do shew the same diligence [constant applied effort] to the full assurance of hope unto the end."

In other words, God is here saying don't be a quitter—finish what you start. "Do not be slothful [or lazy], but be followers of them who through Faith and Patience went on to inherit the promises."

Did you know that patience and faith are twins? And did you know that without patience, your faith will eventually grow weary and faint? It's true! Now, if this occurs, you can bet your bottom dollar that you'll never cash in on any of the promises.

This is why the Bible goes on to say, "For when God made promise to Abraham, because He could swear by no greater, He sware by Himself, saying, 'Surely blessing I will bless thee, and multiplying I will multiply thee. And so, after he had patiently endured [or after He had made patience his friend] he obtained the promise" (Heb. 6:13–15)

In other words, God is saying that you should be fully committed to using your patience, even in the face of all kinds of opposition, and sticking it out till the end. What good is it taking on a project, or having a wilderness experience, or going through all kinds of trials and adversities if, at the end, you don't cash in on the prize or walk away with the promise?

Now here are a few gems concerning patience that I believe will greatly bless you:

1. Patience is the time between the "amen" and the "there it is."
2. Patience is praising God when there's no sign of any answer.
3. Patience is resting upon the great promises of God when the world is laughing at you.
4. Patience is laughing in the face of a storm.
5. Patience is smiling when the devil comes to frown at you.
6. Patience is the key for obtaining God's promises.

By the way, I took God's advice and made patience my friend, and as a result, I eventually finished the house. When I sold it, it became the biggest single paycheck in my entire life. So yes, my friend, in order for you and I to be a possessor and not just a talker and a failed contender, we must not only take these vital tests, but we must also overcome and pass them.

No Longer a Survivor!

Here's something else the Holy Ghost said to me that came as a fresh revelation. He said, "J, you need to know that you're no longer just a survivor, like when you were in the world. Now that you belong to Me, you are more than a conqueror through Jesus, My Son, who daily infuses you with inner strength for whatever challenges lie ahead. And in His matchless name, I have empowered you to conquer and prevail!"

Wow! No longer a survivor! To me that was huge because I had always bragged on being one, but now the Father wanted me to know that Jesus didn't just survive, He triumphed. And now, he was teaching me to adopt that same mentality and do the same.

Concerning Ministry

Now let me share with you some of the things I've learned about ministry. First and foremost, ministry is definitely not for the weak-hearted or for quitters. The truth is, very few ministers ever wind up finishing their course, and even fewer ever finish it with joy.

Is it any wonder that an unprecedented number of ministers are quitting the ministry every month, and almost as many churches are closing their doors all around the world? However, I am fully persuaded that if we will daily apply the Apostle Paul's testimony of 2 Timothy 4:7 to our lives and ministries, the same powerful principles that worked for him will also work for us.

Principle Number One: I Have Fought a Good Fight!

To succeed in life and in ministry will require the fight of your life! All types of wicked unseen forces will be there to try to stop you and do everything within their power to get you to quit. That's just the way it is.

When I think about fighting the good fight, I immediately think of David's victory over Goliath. You remember he defeated the Philistine giant with just a sling and a stone. Then he did something outrageously bold: He ran to where Goliath lay dead, put his foot on his chest, took Goliath's own sword, and chopped his head off with it. Now that's what I call a bad dude! Right? But that was David, because he was anointed to always put on a show.

However, what he did after that is what really blew me away. In 1 Samuel 17:54, we learn that after David chopped Goliath's ugly head off, he picked it up and began carrying it in his hand, boldly displaying it and parading it all the way back to Jerusalem as a trophy of faith and a testimony of his victory over the giant.

When I read this, it occurred to me that it was not the lion and the bear that David slew in the wilderness that brought him from obscurity to notoriety; it was Goliath. You see, the lion and the bear are what God used to get David ready for the day when he would meet Goliath, and it is no different with you and me.

I have discovered that if we're going to do more than just blend into the wall of humanity, and in time simply fade away like so many other people do, we will also have to rise up in the name of Jesus and, by the power and anointing of the Holy Ghost, bring down the Goliaths in our lives.

For example, I can still remember being in a life-and-death struggle with the Goliath of poverty. Do you know him? I do! I remember when I received the revelation that it was Goliath and not my natural circumstances that was standing between me, and God's blessings for my life, family, and ministry.

I can still hear the Spirit of Goliath defying me, trying to terrorize me, yelling at the top of his lungs, "Get through me and you can have the promise! Get through me and you can reap the spoils of war! Get through me and you and your ministry will live! Because if you don't, I'll kill you both!" I can honestly tell you that, for a long, long time, he scared the daylights out of me. But God in his mercy turned it around for me.

Let me tell you how: We had just been blessed with the church in Orange, New Jersey and were barely getting by, when one of my members said to me, "Pastor, I believe we should start a 6:00 a.m. prayer meeting at the church and believe God for a fresh outpouring of the Holy Spirit." I quickly agreed, and so we started praying diligently every morning. Before long, I had the craziest and scariest experience of my life. I remember walking into our old sanctuary on a Wednesday afternoon. Out of nowhere, I came face to face with the principality of the Oranges. A *demonic principality* is the overall ruler of a specific geographical area. In this case, he was the principality ruling over the Oranges. (If you want to know the truth, it was a spirit of Catholicism.) As you well know, Satan's structural order of power flows down from him, to principalities, then to powers, then to the rulers of the darkness of this world, and then they flow all the way down to spiritual wickedness in the high places.

So when this principality, who had ruled over the Oranges for many, many years, manifested himself to me, all I can tell you is that he scared me in a way that I had never been scared before. And although I had cast out many devils from individuals all around the world while traveling with R.W. Shambach, I had never encountered a principality before. After that ordeal, I literally went home, got under the covers, and stayed there for a while, trembling. I'm telling you, that thing had really done a number on me!

I finally got up the next morning and went about my business as usual, but the very next night, as Rev. Fred, who was my first convert, and I were installing the phone system in our new church, he asked me to get the extension cord that was in the platform in the sanctuary.

By then, I had already forgotten about my experience with the principality the night before. But as I walked into the sanctuary that was pitch black and started looking around for this extension cord, bam! To my utter amazement, this crazy principality appeared to me again. And this time it shook me up even worse, to the point that all I wanted to do was run away, quit the ministry, and never go back to that church. At that very moment, it became apparent to me that this principality knew that I was totally terrified of him, and that deep down inside I knew that I was no match for him. All I can say is thank God for the Holy Ghost.

Because even though I was at my wit's end, God knew that all I really needed was one word from Him, and that one word would change everything.

"Prepare your insides for war." Wow! That was the Word of the Lord.

And somehow, deep down inside, I knew what that meant. It meant fast and pray for at least three days and nights, and the Lord would do the rest.

Well, I did exactly that, and on the third day of my fast, after the 6:00 a.m. prayer meeting, after I had dismissed the people, I turned around and there he was once again. Only this time, it was different because I had prepared my insides for war, just like God told me to. This time, I wasn't afraid, *he was!* And right then and there, like a bolt of lightning from heaven, faith struck me, and so instead of running from him as I did in the past, I began running toward him with the mighty name of Jesus in one hand and the Word of God in the other, and *bam!* Down he went! So in the spirit, I did exactly what David did. I ran to where he laid, got on top of him, put my foot on his chest, and cut his ugly head off. Glory to God!

Now, everywhere I go, I display his ugly head as a trophy of faith, a testimony of victory and evidence of his absolute defeat! So, you ask, what is his head? Well, It could be the car I drive, the house I live in, a thriving business, rich relationships, a healthy marriage, peace of mind, souls being saved, backsliders being restored, the gifts of the spirit being manifested through my life, or the amazing blessings on the ministry God has graced me with for the past twenty-eight years.

All I can say is, to God be all the glory!

Later in the book, when I get to the M&Ms for marriage, I will share with you how I brought down the Goliath of divorce and now enjoy heaven on earth in my marriage.

Principle Number Two: I Have Finished My Course

In his parting letter to his son Timothy, Paul writes, "I have finished my course." Paul is not the only one who had a course to finish. Everyone, including you and me, has his or her own course (or race) to run and finish.

Another thing I've learned is that not everyone who starts finishes. I have known so many amazing people who started out with a bang. I thought, *Surely, they're going to shake the world with the gospel.* However, for one reason or another, in times of great pressure, they fell away, and instead of bringing God glory, they brought him much shame. This is why I believe preparation time is never wasted time, and God's boot camp or school of the Holy Spirit is so incredibly vital.

As far as I am concerned, this was the difference between King Saul and King David. When God chose Saul, he went right into the ministry without any training or preparation, and the results were tragic. I believe that, due to this lack of preparation, when great pressure eventually came on Saul, he simply couldn't handle it. Why? Because he had never been through the school of the Holy Spirit to receive the kind of preparation that would have gotten him ready for that level of pressure.

As a result, when the pressure of that level of leadership that he had never been prepared for came on him, it simply overwhelmed him and eventually drove him mad. Tragically, at the end of his life, because of his utter disobedience, when he tried to contact God, God simply refused to talk to him. So finally, he turned to the Witch of Endor for help and direction, and that move was the last nail in the coffin and the final act that sealed his doom. As we learn from the scripture, King Saul committed suicide, having never finished his course. The Bible simply says that King Saul died in the midst of the battle. How tragic!

On the other hand, it took David more than thirteen long years of intense training and preparation in the school of the Holy Spirit before he was ever ready to sit upon his kingly throne and rule Israel. I truly believe that's what made the difference.

Let me share with you a principle that the late Reverend Benson Idahosa taught me many years ago that has greatly impacted my life: "Prayerful preparation prevents poor performance." I call it the five P's necessary for success.

This principle, for many years now, has been one of the foundation stones in my life and ministry, and it has taught me the importance of being ready, in season and out of season, for life's unexpected challenges and also godly accomplishments. I've learned that what the world calls *luck* is simply being ready when opportunities knock. Then, years later, I discovered another truth that Jesus Himself taught me when I was in the throes of despair and ready to give up: "Man ought always to pray, and not to faint!" (Luke 18:1). The Amplified Bible says it this way: "… man ought always to pray and not to turn coward (faint, lose heart, and give up)."

Back then, when the enemy did his best to get me to give up, I realized I had two options: pray or give up, pray or turn coward, pray or lose heart. Thank God I chose to pray and not to give up, and in time, God gave me a great, great victory.

As a rule of thumb, I believe it is vital that you spend the first part of your day with God in prayer. In other words, before you ever talk with anyone else, have your daily talks with God. I call it putting first things first, which is equivalent to Proverbs 3:6: "In all of your ways acknowledge Him and He will direct your paths." The message Bible reads this way: "In everything you do, put God first." Now, if you will do this every day—put God first—God's promise to you is, "He will direct you" and "crown your efforts with success." I think that's an awesome promise! Don't you?

After this simple prayer, I simply ask Him to fill my reservoir with his wisdom and with the power necessary to meet all the unexpected challenges that life may bring my way that day. Throughout the rest of the day, I simply pray in the Holy Ghost at will and as often as I can, because the truth is, I don't really know what's around the corner like He does, and on top of that, I can't really see the pitfalls and the snares of the enemy like He can; that's why I always pray in the spirit. Here's another important thing I've discovered: When I pray in the spirit, I am releasing God's unlimited potential for future possibilities in my life and ministry that I might not even be aware exist.

Lastly, here's another principle I practice continuously. This one's called *mercy*. Mercy is my only alternative when I have run out of options. Honestly, there have been times when I've been so depleted and battle fatigued that I didn't have the will nor the strength to pray. This doesn't happen often, but when it does, I just throw myself at the feet of Jesus and simply cry out for mercy.

Blind Bartimaeus cried out for mercy, and Jesus gave him sight!

The ten lepers in Luke 17 cried out for mercy and were healed!

When King David fell with Bathsheba, he cried, "Lord, have mercy on me, for I have sinned." And the Lord had mercy on him and forgave David his sins.

Oh, my friend, remember: *Only the guilty need mercy!*

So if you are at your wit's end, for whatever reason, you too can cry out for mercy right now, and God will grant it to you, for He delights in mercy!

Principle Number Three: I Have Kept the Faith

Finally, in the scripture that we are looking at, Paul writes, "I have kept the faith." Now why is faith so important? Consider this. Do you remember when Jesus informs Peter, "Simon, Simon, Satan has desired to have you, that he might sift you as wheat. But I have prayed for you, that your faith fail not" (Luke 22:31)?

To me, it might seem better if Jesus had said, "Simon, Simon,

Satan has desired to have you that he might sift you as wheat, but don't worry about a thing, because I have already broken his power over your life and prayed you through. So Peter, don't give it another thought. Satan won't be bothering you anymore."

But no, that's not what happened, and that's not what Jesus prayed. Instead, he told Peter, "Simon, I have prayed for you, that your faith fail not." Wow! Here we discover that as long as we are in this world, even though Jesus is personally praying for us, it doesn't necessarily mean that we are going to be spared or delivered from having to go through difficulties and trying times. It does mean, however, that if we don't lose our faith, no matter what we go through, eventually, our faith will help us find our way back, just like Peter, and put the devil where he belongs—and that's under our feet!

Sadly enough, I know a lot of people who mock faith. Yet, when I look at their lives, it is evident that they have no clue what faith is nor how to use it.

1. What Is Bible Faith?

Faith is confidence in God and His Word. Bottom line: it is faith in God's faithfulness.

Faith is believing God's Word. Thinking like it is so. Talking like it is so. Acting like it is so. Rejoicing like it is so, in the face of no apparent visible proof. Because if you can see it, or feel it, or taste it, then it isn't faith.

Faith is simply putting God's Word first, no matter how you feel, and no matter what things look like.

Now, for the icing on the cake, we go to Hebrews 11:6, where we learn that without faith, it is *impossible* to please Him. You see, I have discovered that nothing brings more joy to the heart of the Father than when we believe Him. And nothing makes him sadder than when we doubt Him.

So the bottom line is, if we really want to please the Father, we must walk by faith and not by sight.

2. How Does Faith Come?

Faith does not come by fasting, or by dancing in the aisles of the church, or by shouting and falling out in between the pews. No, faith comes by hearing, and hearing by the Word (or *rhema*) of God.

I don't know what you're facing today. You might even be ready to give up on life itself. But God told me to tell you: Don't quit now, because you have faith—world-overcoming faith, mountain-moving faith—and your faith will turn it around for you.

Listen to me,

- It was faith that healed the woman with the issue of blood. (Mark 5:34)
- It was faith that delivered the woman's daughter who was possessed by a demon. (Matt. 15:28)
- It was faith that gave sight to blind Bartimaeus. (Mark 10:46–52)
- It was faith that raised Jairus' daughter from the dead. (Matt. 9:18–26)
- It was faith that caused Peter to walk on water. (Matt. 14:29)
- It was faith that made the ten lepers whole. (Luke 17:14)
- It was faith that healed the man at the gate called beautiful. (Acts 3:2)
- It was faith that empowered Stephen to do signs, wonders, and miracles among the people. (Acts 6:8)
- t was faith that healed the crippled man in Lystra.

No wonder Jesus told Martha, "'Said I not unto thee, that If You Would Believe, you would See the Glory of God?' … And with that, he cried with a loud voice [because faith is voice-activated] 'Lazarus, come forth!' And he that was dead, came forth, hopping out of that grave, alive, to the glory of God!" John 11:40, 43.

If you have to lose something, go ahead and lose your coat, just like Joseph did. But don't you ever let go of your faith. Why? Because faith is what will get you back your coat. Faith is what will help you find your way back to God. Faith is what will empower you to be healed, to be delivered, and to receive your miracle from God.

And never ever forget this: The seasons of your life don't change when you have a need. No sir, they will change when you decide to use your faith.

So use it or lose it!

In closing, let me leave you with a rich nugget an old preacher once gave me when I first started in the ministry. He said, "Son, if what you believe isn't worth dying for, then what you believe isn't worth living for." I fully agree! What about you?

Today, I decree over you, that you will prevail and fulfill all your God-given dreams and finish your course with joy, in Jesus' name.

Chapter 7

The Seventh
M—Mistakes

> Some people refuse to bend when someone corrects
> them. Eventually they will break, and there will be
> no one to repair the damage.
>
> —Proverbs 29:1 (ERV)

Today, while looking back on all the mistakes I've made, I thank God that Jesus is merciful, and Our heavenly Father is the God of a second chance!

So as I begin to share my thoughts on mistakes, let me first encourage you by saying that we are learners and not losers. In every situation, we either win or learn.

Now, here are some of the mistakes I have made.

1. I got married at the tender age of fourteen: Talk about mistakes!

But you know what they say: If you play with fire, you'll get burned. Well, I did, and by that I mean that by the time I was fourteen years old, I had gotten a young girl pregnant. Before long, her father found out about it, came looking for me, showed up in my house, found me, grabbed me by the throat, put a butcher knife to my stomach, and said, "If you don't marry her, I'll cut you from one side to the other, until all your guts are hanging out and you bleed out. Now, what are you going to do?"

I said, "I will do whatever you say!"

So that's how that went down. I had no other choice! Yet God in his mercy has used my testimony to bless many people around the world.

2. I also made the mistake of thinking I could play the Hammond organ.

Man, was that ever a mistake! I was the worst at it! (I didn't want to play it, but my friends insisted.) Now let me tell you how that all changed: One day, my friends and I were trying to move my Hammond C3 organ down from the second floor, when all of a sudden, it slipped out of someone's hands and fell all the way down to the bottom of those stairs, breaking it all apart. I can still see and hear my precious father crying in agony and my friends screaming, "Oh no! Oh no! How could this happen? J, we're so sorry!" But all the while, deep down inside, I kept shouting, "Yes! Yes! Yes!" Well, that glorious day when my C3 organ was shattered to pieces, it broke the chains that had been binding me for a long time. Finally, I could once again sing, "Free at last, free at last, thank God Almighty I'm free at last!" And sure enough, from that unforgettable moment, my organ-playing days were over. The truth is, I felt like a man who had served his prison sentence well and at last had been set free.

3. Another huge mistake I can clearly remember is trusting people who had not earned it or proven themselves.

You talk about a painful mistake and a difficult learning experience! The first thing I learned was that trust and respect are not to be freely given away like candy. They must be earned. When I realized this, I had to make up in my mind that, going forward, I would have to learn to qualify people for access into my inner circle of life, because not everyone qualified, and not everyone was worthy to walk hand in hand with me.

Furthermore, I had to look closely at who was already in my inner circle and realize that many of them never belonged there to begin with, and that some who were with me in the present definitely did not belong in my future, because just as sure as seasons in our life change, so do people.

Jesus's Relationships

I didn't know that when it came to relationships, Jesus himself operated on five different levels:

A. The first level was the multitudes, or those people who, for the most part, he never met face to face. He simply ministered to them and only touched them at a distance.

B. The second level was the seventy, which he sent out to preach and cast out devils.
   Those, I'm sure, He spent more time with, teaching and pouring Himself into them. And although he was closer to them, they were not in His inner circle.

C. The third level, were the twelve, to whom he expounded the Word and ordained as apostles. I'm sure these were the ones He spent the most time with, because they were His inner circle.

D. The fourth level was the three—Peter, James, and John.
   His relationship with them was deeper still than with the other nine. These he would occasionally take with him on special missions, like when he went up to the mountain of transfiguration.

Another example was when Jesus raised the twelve-year-old girl from the dead whose father was the ruler of a synagogue. Mark tells us, "As soon as Jesus heard the word that was spoken, He saith unto the ruler of the synagogue, be not afraid; only believe. And he suffered no man to follow him, save Peter, and James, and John the brother of James" (Mark 5:36–37). I believe these were the three whom He was personally grooming to take the lead after his departure.

E. On the fifth and most intimate level, there was only one: John.

Amazingly enough, John was the only one at the last supper who laid his head on Jesus's heart. To me, this is so sad because there are so many people who long for His blessings, His power, or His favor, but very few ever really want His heart. And honestly, it's no different with you and me. This is why one of the most difficult lessons I have had to learn is that not everyone who is around me wants my heart either. They may want my money or my favor, my help or my company, but unfortunately, not my heart. This is why I'm urging you to begin qualifying people for access to your life and stop allowing everyone who knocks on your heart's door to freely come in. Remember: Not everyone is worthy or qualifies!

Now let me share with you a few qualifiers. This list is not all-inclusive, but here are a few. If you come up with more, please share them with me.

Acceptance

Let me put it to you this way: Go where you are celebrated and not just tolerated.

In Matthew 10:14, Jesus instructs the disciples, "and whosoever shall not receive you, nor hear your words, when ye depart out of that house or city, shake off the dust of your feet." The dust on their feet was symbolic of the spirit of rejection they had just experienced. So what Jesus was literally telling them was, "Don't you dare allow this spirit to cling to you any longer. Before you go anywhere else, break its power over you and shake it off; then move on!"

I believe you will always bloom where you are planted, welcomed, and celebrated, and wither where you are rejected and tolerated. The late John Osteen would always say, follow after peace, favor, and love … I believe, these are post signs to your success!

Now here are a few things about rejection I believe you ought to know:

1. Rejection is a spirit.
2. The spirit of rejection is like a bad virus—at times highly contagious!
3. Rejection is often the seedbed or open door for the spirit of anger to emerge!
4. Dust is one of the delicacies demons feed on—it is a type of rejection!

And the Lord God said unto the serpent, "Because thou hast done this, thou art cursed above all cattle, and above every beast of the field; upon thy belly shalt thou go, and dust shalt thou eat all the days of thy life" (Genesis 3:14) This is why Jesus said, after his disciples were rejected, to "shake the dust off of your feet" (Matt. 10:14). Today, I charge you to walk in freedom and in victory over rejection. "Shake it off"!

Respect

If someone doesn't respect you, that relationship, no matter how hard you try, is not going anywhere, because you can't be cutting each other up with unkind words or put-downs and then expect to have a healthy relationship. It just won't work!

Someone once said that in order for any relationship to be strong and healthy, there must of necessity exist a mutual respect. Again, I fully agree!

The moment disrespect continues to occur in a relationship, that relationship is headed for chaos and big trouble, or most likely is over. My advice to you is to bow out *gracefully!* Here's a few quotes I love:

1. "Respect! Give it to get it."
2. "Show respect even to people who don't deserve it—not as a reflection of their character, but as a reflection of yours."
3. "Give the gift of your absence to those who do not appreciate your presence."

How about Trust?

Here's the number-one thing I always ask myself when I think of allowing someone to come close to me: Do I feel safe with this person? Can I trust this person with my heart, with my secrets, with my fears, and so on? Because if this person has not proven himself or herself worthy, and I still give him or her access to my heart, then I'm asking for serious trouble. This is why I always say that welcoming people into our hearts and lives without the leading of the Holy Spirit can be extremely dangerous. Again, we must learn to qualify people for access and qualify the soil around us before we plant the seed of our life in it.

Acknowledged Mistakes

It is important that you understand that mistakes, when acknowledged, many times become the great teachers in the never-ending school of life. I believe mistakes are what God often uses to enlarge us and many times teach us lessons that last a lifetime. I am convinced that these are the lessons that can help us successfully navigate our way throughout life.

I have also discovered that mistakes, when acknowledged, can actually become part of the process that God uses to impart wisdom to us. At the same time, we should be chiseling away at potential flaws in our lives that, if not acknowledged and repented of, can later be used against us by the enemy.

Here is something else I've learned: If a person, after being corrected a number of times, refuses to acknowledge an error and continues to make the same mistake over and over again, then it's no longer a mistake. It has become a choice. And many times that type of willful ignorance is a clear indication and explanation of a person's character and flaws.

The truth is, we are what we repeatedly do. For example, you may make the mistake of gossiping about your pastor and his wife, or anyone else for that matter, and suddenly the spirit of God convicts you or someone confronts you with the truth. Instead of acknowledging that you have done wrong, you choose to ignore it and continue gossiping. Now you are gossiper! Because if it were a mistake that was brought to your attention, you would first acknowledge you did wrong. Secondly, you would repent and ask God for mercy and forgiveness. Finally, you would humbly ask God to grant you sufficient grace to help you once and for all learn from that mistake so that you never did it again.

If I'm rubbing the cat's fur the wrong way, just let the cat turn around. Remember, we're learners, not losers.

And remember, this book is not for condemnation but for information, and my intention for writing this book is not to push you down but to pull you up!

Now, are you aware that everyone in the Bible except for Jesus made mistakes? Oh yes, they did. For example,

1. Adam made the mistake of not exercising his authority over the devil in the Garden, but thank God the last Adam (Jesus) did, and as a result, crushed him under his feet!
2. Eve made the mistake of engaging in a conversation with the great intruder and enemy of her soul, when she should have rebuked him.
3. Noah made the mistake of getting drunk on his own success!

4. Abraham made the mistake of lying about his wife. And had it not been for God's mercy and divine intervention, he could have lost it all.

5. Isaac made the mistake of allowing his base appetite to control his better judgment when Jacob deceitfully came asking for his blessing. And instead of going with what he knew deep down in his gut, he checked with his senses and his senses deceived him.

6. Jacob made the mistake of trusting his uncle Laban. He soon found out that you always reap what you sow, and the conman always gets conned.

7. Moses kept making the mistake of always losing his temper, and eventually it cost him dearly. Just remember: Anger is the open-back-door policy the devil uses to steal your peace, destroy your relationships, and kill your future. Anger has no friends.

8. Joshua dropped his guard, became lazy, and made the mistake of entering into a covenant with a deceitful tribe. Here's wisdom! Before you ever make a major decision in life, make sure you first check down inside yourself.
What do you check for? You check for either the presence or the absence of peace. In other words, if you have a check or an uneasy feeling or an unrest inside, then it's a no!

On the other hand, if you have a witness of peace or a joyful agreement or a warm sensation inside you, then it's a yes! Listen as Paul says, "… and let the Peace [or soul harmony which comes] from Christ *rule* [or act as an umpire continually] in your hearts (deciding and settling with finality all questions that arise in your minds)." (Col. 3:15 AMPC) I can't even begin to tell you how many times this simple revelation has saved me from making drastic decisions that would have resulted in grave consequences.

9. Samson made the mistake of thinking he could trust Delilah and not pay the price. Take it from me, never trust a scorpion!

10. Joseph made the mistake of telling his dream to his half-brothers. I've discovered that most half-brothers never have your best interest at heart because they are jealous.

11. David made the mistake of staying home at a time when kings were supposed to go forth to battle, and it turned out to be the most grievous mistake in his life.

12. Solomon made the mistake of not heeding God's warnings concerning strange women. I guess he forgot to practice what he preached (mainly, that wisdom is the principal thing).

13. Peter made the mistake of denying the Lord Jesus. Yet, at the end of his life, when he was about to be crucified, he requested to be crucified upside down because, he said, "I'm not worthy to die like my Lord."

14. Saul of Tarsus, before he became the great Apostle Paul, made the mistake of thinking that persecuting Christians was the right thing to do. Think about it—one wrong thought had him torturing and killing innocent people.

We have all made mistakes. But when we acknowledge them and repent, mistakes can become part of the growth and development process in our lives, which God will many times use as stepping stones to take us to the next level. But for those who refuse to learn from their mistakes and who harden their hearts to correction, mistakes become their tombstones. This is why I plead with you to keep your heart tender and pliable to correction.

Don't just listen to me; let's see what God has to say about it.

He, that is often reproved (and) Hardeneth his neck, shall Suddenly be destroyed, and that without remedy. (Prov. 29:1)

Now listen to this same scripture in the message Bible:

> Those, who Hate Discipline and only get more stubborn, There'll come a day when life Tumbles in and They Break, but by then it'll be too late to help them."

Wow!

Have you ever asked, "How did this happen? How could this happen?" especially when people you knew who looked like they had it all together suddenly got taken out, or out of nowhere and for no apparent reason, things began happening to them that could not be explained? I have! And for a long, long time, these type of things really troubled me. The truth is that it wasn't until I began to receive insight into scriptures like these that I clearly understood that God was not to blame, and if the truth be told, you never really know what goes on behind closed doors. Now ain't that the truth!

The bottom line is this: If you want to survive and become a winner on the stage of life, you must develop both the hide of a rhinoceros and the heart of a butterfly.

Listen as God speaks to us in Isaiah 41:10 in the Amplified Bible. Here, He tells us, "Fear not (for there is nothing to fear) for I am with you. I will *strengthen* and *harden you to difficulties.*" Here's what I call having the hide of a rhinoceros, and man, don't we all need this? Because as long as you have breath in your lungs, ready or not, troubles and difficulties will come. But here's the good news: If you dare ask God to strengthen and harden you to difficulties, like He said he would, He will!

But that's only one side. The other side of that coin is a *tender heart*, a heart that's pliable, teachable, and moldable. This is why Hebrews 3:15 warns us, "Today if ye will hear his voice, harden not your heart."

Every time I read this, I am reminded of the scripture my wife would always quote to me after an argument before we went to bed. "Be ye angry and sin not."

Now here's my personal translation of Ephesians 4:26–27: "It's all right to be angry and let your frustrations air out for a while rather than holding them in, hardening your heart, and later on using your anger as fuel for revenge." So she would say, "J, before we go to bed, let's resolve our anger and forgive one another. Let's not stay angry. Let's not go to bed angry. Let's not give the devil that kind of foothold in our life." I must admit I learned this truth the hard way, and now I pass it on to you!

So it is always our personal responsibility and choice to remain tender and pliable to God's correction in order that we might experience a healthy, disciplined, and victorious life. That's what I call the heart of a butterfly. This is why I'm always asking God to keep me tender and keep me sweet, and now I always do my best to resolve my anger before I ever go to bed, and so should you!

Let me close this chapter by sharing a story I will never forget. This is an experience I had while visiting a wax factory in Pennsylvania. There, I saw a man easily manipulating a piece of wax with his hands. This guy literally bent the wax, squeezed it, and molded and shaped it in every possible way. Now here's the amazing thing: the piece of wax never broke. So I asked him, "How are you doing that?"

He replied, "Oh, it's simple. As long as I keep this piece of wax by this lamp, the wax will remain pliable and easy to handle. But if I removed it from the presence and warmth of the lamp and then try to mold and shape it, then it would immediately break." It hit me immediately: It is no different with us. As long as we stay close to God's heart (the Word) and his presence (His Spirit), we will stay soft and pliable. However, the minute we begin to move or drift away, we will once again begin to get hard and become unmanageable.

Let me leave you with Proverbs 29:1 in the ERV translation:

"Some people refuse to bend when someone corrects them. Eventually they will break, and there will be no one to repair the damage."

Today, I decree that you are a learner and not a loser! You are pliable in the Master's hands, and in the name of Jesus, you will fulfill all his plans for your life!

Chapter 8

The Eighth M—Marriage

Someone said, "The closest you will ever get to hell without ever going there is a bad marriage. And the closest you will ever get to heaven without ever really going there is a good marriage." I know that's right!

After forty-three years of marriage and counting, I can honestly say that I've been on both sides of that saying. Today, I'm so glad my wife and I are experiencing heaven on earth, but it has not always been that way. I remember the days when I dreaded just the thought of going home. I would look for every excuse possible to stay out late or to travel.

You see, in my mind, my home had become a war zone. It just seemed as if we were always arguing about something, never realizing that all this arguing had turned into a vicious stone-throwing contest that was inflicting great pain and causing irreplaceable damage to our lives—and, may I add, without ever realizing it, this madness was also greatly impacting the lives of our children.

This is why I will never forget the open vision I had while speaking to a gathering of young students in a Christian grammar school in Nutley, New Jersey. Suddenly I was in the spirit, and to my amazement, I found myself inside a house where a husband and wife were arguing and screaming at each other at the top of their lungs. In an instant, the scene shifted, and I began seeing through one of the walls of the house into a small bedroom where a young girl was lying on her bed, listening to all that was going on between her mother and father. I could clearly see and hear her crying and shaking like a leaf. When suddenly, God spoke to me and said, "Do you see what's happening? Can you see what this arguing is doing?" In my heart, I answered, "Yes, Lord." Then he replied, "Her security and sense of safety, which her parents have always provided, has now been stripped from her, and in its place, confusion, fear, and anger have begun to penetrate her. And if she doesn't get the proper help soon, she might never recover."

Is it any wonder why so many young people grow up seriously damaged on the inside? Now here's the sad part: Many of them will never really know where or how it all started. This is why, in our homes, we must guard against pride and stay out of strife at all cost. Please hear my heart and know that my purpose in sharing this vision is not for condemnation but for information, and in order that we should no longer continue to be ignorant of the devil's devices.

Now let me share with you a scripture concerning strife that really put the fear of God in me. "But if ye bite and devour one another, take heed that ye be not consumed one of another" (Gal. 5:15). The Good News Testament puts it this way: "But if you act like wild animals, hurting and tearing up each other, then watch out, or you will completely devour and destroy one another." Now, can you see it?

Is this crazy or what? Can you even begin to imagine that something like this can possibly be going on behind closed doors, especially in Christian homes?

Well, whether you believe it or not, it does happen! And it often happens with the least likely people. The reason I know is that this went on in my own home, and I hated it, because when I was young, I was taught that the home was supposed to be a place of refuge, a shelter from life's storms, a strong tower, my hiding place. Sad to say, but that was not the case—not at all.

Instead, my home became a breeding ground for hostility and demon activity, a place where strife reigned. This is why James's teaching on the subject became such an eye opener for me. Listen to it.

> "For where envying and strife is, there is confusion (war – unrests) and every evil work present." James 3:16

Now think about it. God tells us that if there is strife in your home or in your office or even in your church, there—wherever *there* is—is confusion, war, unrest, and every evil work present! Wow! Is it any wonder why the devil works overtime to get us to reach for that bait? Personally, I believe it's because he knows that what Jesus said in Matthew 12:25 is true: "Every kingdom, [not some. But every kingdom …

That also can mean, every home, church, or nation] that fights against itself will eventually fall and come to ruins. "

Now can you understand why so many homes are falling apart, being destroyed, and not surviving? But there's good news! The Goliath of strife—or any other Goliath for that matter—can be stopped, brought down, and defeated in Jesus' name. I am a witness!

I have learned another about strife that might help you. Strife, as you well know, is a deadly spiritual poison. But what I didn't know was that strife always creates an "open-back-door policy," which allows the enemy to interfere with every other single area in our life. In other words, you could be doing a million good things—and by that I mean things like praying, singing in the choir, tithing, and giving offerings, or perhaps you're a stellar Christian in your job and community—but if at the same time, you have strife in your life, the devil, through that "open-back-door policy," will then have the right to eat away at your finances, your health, your ministry, and even your relationships.

Now here's the sad thing: Unless, we humble ourselves and put an end to that strife, there will be nothing God can do about it.

I once heard the late Reverend David Wilkerson say, "When my ministry gets into financial trouble, I immediately know strife has crept into my staff."

Reverend Kenneth Copeland taught, "The one thing I will not tolerate in my ministry is strife." Why? Because he knows that strife will hinder prayers from being answered, dry up finances, and quench the divine flow of God's anointing in life.

This is why I always warn people to stay out of strife at all cost. But just in case I'm too late, and you're presently involved in some kind of strife, this is what I encourage you to do: Humble yourself. Go and make peace with the other person as best you can, no matter what, because like I always say, I'd much rather eat a spoonful of dirt right now in humility, and obey God, than to have a truckload full of dirt poured on my head later on because of my pride. So don't put it off; humble yourself now. Strike while the anointing is hot, and get it done.

Remember! Nothing is worth you losing your peace and victory over. Nothing!

Here's something else the Lord recently revealed to me about strife. He said, "When it comes to the art of communicating, the most important thing is not so much what a person says as what a person hears. And how a person hears is all based on an individual's filtering system. This is why Jesus said, 'Take heed or be careful what you hear.' But that's not all. He also warned us to be careful *how* we hear."

The Lord then said to me, "A person's filtering system is mainly based on how one has been raised and on what one has experienced throughout one's lifetime.

It is literally what helps a person interpret what they hear and also what they see."

Now, when I thought about this, I realized that even in the natural, this is exactly what will happen if you attempt to pour clean water into a cup through a dirty filter.

The only difference here is that this is taking place in the spirit.

If your filtering system is negative or twisted, then, for the most part, what you hear and see will be interpreted as being negative or twisted. The opposite is also true. It's pretty much like two different individuals looking at the same glass of water. You ask them both, "What do you see?" The one with a negative filtering system will say, "I see a glass that's half empty." However, the person with a positive filtering system will say, "I see a glass that's half full." They both see the same glass, but they interpret it differently.

Why? It all depends on a person's filtering system—the way people are capable of interpreting what they hear and see.

Take my marriage, for example. Little did I know that every time my wife and I sat down to talk to each other and try to make peace, by the time my words—which were intended to do good and bring peace—had passed through that filtering system of strife that our constant arguing had created, they had been twisted into something that I never said or meant. This is why I always say that ignorance is such a lofty price to pay.

You see, no one had ever told me that the words you speak are what attract spirits, whether angels or demons. For example, in the tenth chapter of the book of Daniel, we discover that Daniel's fasting and praying brought Michael the Archangel with a message from the Lord. "Then said he (the Angel) unto me, Fear not, Daniel: for from the first day that thou didst set thine heart to understand, and to chasten thyself before thy God, thy *words* were heard, and I am come *for thy words*."

Notice that the Angel didn't come for Daniel's fasting, but he came for his *words*. This scripture helped me to see that whenever words are spoken—whether they are words of life or death, blessing or cursing; whether they're spoken in a bedroom, in an office, or even in a church—those very words give the legal right for unseen forces, whether God, the devil, angels, or demons, to take up residence and manifest themselves.

No wonder my wife and I had such a difficult time communicating, especially after we had had a big blowout in our house. The truth is that it wasn't until the Lord revealed this to me that I began to understand that our constant strife was legally inviting all kinds of evil spirits to invade our home and allowing them to create a dirty and a twisted filtering system between us that would interfere with every attempt we ever made to get things right. Every time I tried to communicate with my wife in order to get things right, by the time my words, which were meant to bring peace, reached her ears, after having passed through that dirty and twisted filtering system these evil spirits had created through our strife, she would hear something I never said, and something I never meant. So instead of our conversation producing peace, it would just explode into another big argument and add more wood to the fire.

Honestly, I can still hear myself saying to her, "No, Gale, that's not what I said. This is what I said." And, "No, Gale, that's not what I meant. This is what I meant." But most of the time, it was to no avail. And truthfully, it was no different with her, because every time she attempted to make peace with me, I would also hear something she didn't really say or mean. No wonder God's Word tells us, "my people are being destroyed for a lack of knowledge" Hosea 4:6.

Now that I know better, before we ever have a meaningful conversation, I make sure I first bind up and drive out of the room every spirit that is contrary to the Holy Spirit, in Jesus' name, and loose the presence and power of the Holy Spirit to have preeminence.

Then, after doing this, I simply lift up my voice and sing Him a love song, or I'll just begin thanking him and praising him for His tender mercy, His amazing grace, and His great love. Why? Because "He inhabits, or dwells in the midst of the praises of his people" (Psalm 22:3 AMPC). Or like the Hebrew says, ["He will come down and set up his throne, where ever the praises of his people are offered."] Isn't that awesome?

Kicking Out the Troublemakers

Knowing what I know now, if you were to ask me what I believe is the biggest challenge facing marriages today, I would have to say that, besides the lack of money, it would be strife and division.

Listen to this word of wisdom from Proverbs 22:10 in the Message Bible:

"Kick out the troublemakers (strife and division) and things will quiet down; you need a break from bickering and griping, so that you can recover."

The easy-to-read translation says it this way: "Get rid of the proud who laugh at what is right [to me, this refers to the spirits of strife and division], and trouble will leave with them. Then, all arguments and insults will end." Isn't that awesome?

I believe the biggest troublemakers in many homes today are the spirits of strife and division, and unless someone is willing and able to rise up in Jesus' name and kick them out, they will continue to cause havoc in both your life and your home.

You know what they say: If you invite the devil for lunch, he will always bring his pajamas. In other words, once he has been invited through strife and division into your home, he won't leave until someone kicks him out!

Now here's what I did, and I encourage you to do the same:

1. First, I humbled myself and asked God to have mercy on me and forgive me and cleanse me with the blood of Jesus from all my sins and wrongdoing.

2. Before I dealt with anyone else, I bound up the spirits of strife and division and broke their power over my own life first, in Jesus' name.

3. I rose up in the realm of the Spirit and kicked out the troublemakers of strife and division from my home and marriage, in Jesus' name, and forbade them to come back again.

4. I began applying Proverbs 20:3, which says, "It is an honor for a man to cease from strife: but every fool will continue to argue and fight." So I began confessing over myself. Any fool can start an argument, but I'm not a fool. I am a wise man. Therefore, I will do the honorable thing and put an end to strife in my home and life right now. And because I am a peace maker, a peace lover, and a peace keeper in Jesus's name, strife no longer has a place in me or in my home.

5. Then I began to praise and thank God for delivering my wife and me out from under the power and dominion of darkness and for transporting us into the kingdom of his precious Son Jesus Christ, the Prince of Peace!

6. Lastly, I began practicing Proverbs 26:20, which teaches us, "Where no wood is, there! There! *There!* the fire goes out." From this scripture, I realized that it was vital that I learn to walk in love and stay out of strife at all cost, in Jesus' name, because my marriage and my future depended on it. And man, I'm so glad I did!

A Healed Marriage!

Before closing this chapter out, I would like to share one more principle with you,

one that I believe will be a great source of strength and blessing to you. It illustrates the principle of kindness.

I will never forget that night. It was during a time when my wife and I were both at our wit's end. The atmosphere in our home was so thick with hostility that you could almost cut it with a knife. I was getting ready to walk out the door, when suddenly, Gale approached me and asked if it was possible for us to sit and talk at least one more time. Immediately I thought, *Now, what can possibly be said that hasn't already been said?* But God in His mercy intervened, and so we sat down and talked for a while.

I can honestly say that, for the first ten minutes, it felt as if we were once again just wasting our time. We had been around this old mountain quite a few times before. So I informed her, "I have to go."

She responded, "Let me ask you just one more question, and please think about it before you answer me. Can we please try again? Because I believe the Lord said our marriage will work if we will simply start being kind to one another. J, can we please try?" She then added, "I'm willing! Are you?"

I admit that, at that moment, all I really felt was a deep anger raging inside me. Yet at the same time, I knew that if there was any chance for our marriage to get back on track and glorify God, we had to try at least one more time, and this time we needed to give it all we had. Well, little did I know that God was going to use our simple acts of kindness to dispel the darkest night in our lives!

To be perfectly honest, when I first started to put into practice this principle of kindness, I didn't always feel like being kind. For example, one night, walking into our living room where she was sitting and in spite of all the anger and pain I was still feeling, I asked her if she would like for me to make her a nice cup of hot tea. She responded, "Yes, that would be so nice. Thank you."

I'll never forget what happened next. As I turned from her and began walking toward the kitchen to make her the tea, I began murmuring under my breath and making fun of her by making negative facial expressions that were not nice. (I'm sure you know what I mean!)

But believe it or not, right then and there, instead of the Holy Ghost condemning me, He began revealing to me that kindness is not a feeling; it is rather an act. Doesn't the Bible teach us that love is kind, and that *love* is an action word?

It took a long, long time before my feelings started catching up to my actions, because I was all broken up inside. But here's the thing that I believe broke the devil's back: I kept putting forth the effort and practicing kindness, no matter how I felt.

Now here is what I want you to see. If I had waited for God to heal me first, before I began to act it out, I don't believe my marriage would have had a chance. But thank God I didn't yield to my feelings, but rather pushed all the way through to victory. I simply obeyed, and as a result, today our marriage is a living testimony to the fact that when all else had failed, our little acts of kindness are what God used mightily to help our marriage through the healing process that we so desperately needed and to get us back on track.

So why curse the darkness when you can light a candle? In other words, instead of allowing your present situation to swallow you up and ruin your life, why don't you do something about it? Do what I did. Try a little tenderness and a good dose of kindness every day and see what God will do!

Listen to me. If God is speaking to you, don't keep putting it off. Retaliate against your feelings and start being kind, because if the enemy can get you to harden your heart, it will be almost impossible for your marriage to survive, and I don't believe you really want that. By the way, this principle will work not only in your marriage, but in every other relationship in your life.

Here's something else I've learned on my glorious journey: Many times in a marriage, pain never really goes away. Pain has to be released! In other words, you must be willing to give it to God and let it go before the healing process can ever begin.

I would like to share a precious nugget I once heard Oral Roberts say: "A song is not a song until you sing it. A bell is not a bell until you ring it. And love is not love until you give it away." In other words, love is not love until you act on it. Simple, right? Now go do it!

This simple testimony is not just one of survival, but one of triumph! If you will receive it, this is the kind of spirit I now impart to you in Jesus' name. Receive it! Now give God the glory!

In Closing, let me share with you five of my favorite daily prayers!

1. **Father, divinely inspire me!**

   Father, I ask you to daily inspired me to write, to create, to preach, to teach, to sing, and to minister up under your anointing by the power of the Holy Spirit, in prediction and simple discourse, in Jesus' mighty name. Amen!

2. **Father, divinely enlighten me!**

   Father, I ask you to daily light my candle and enlighten my darkness. Father, flood me with knowledge of Your will, Your ways, Your Word, and Your wisdom, in Jesus's mighty name. Amen!

3. **Father, divinely empower me!**

   Father, I ask you to empower me with the gifts of the spirit throughout this day as you see fit. Blow upon my garden, O God, and let the spices thereof flow out in Jesus's name. Father, manifest Yourself through me today with the gifts of power [special faith, gifts of healings, the working of miracles], with the gifts of revelation [the gift of the word of wisdom, the gift of the of word of knowledge, the gift of discerning of spirits], and the gifts of utterance [the gift of prophecy, the gift of tongues, and the interpretation of tongues] as the right opportunities present themselves. Father, do it all for Your glory, in Jesus' name. Amen!

4. **Father, divinely energize me!**

   Father, today I ask you to divinely energize me with resurrection life and power by the Holy Ghost. I boldly confess the Lord is the strength of my life and my portion for ever and ever, and I will go in the strength of the Lord. Father, I will make known Your strength to this generation and to those that are to come. Today, I boldly confess I can do all things through Christ who strengthens me, and I am ready for anything, equal to anything, through Christ who daily infuses me with inner strength in the inner man, in Jesus's mighty name. Amen!

5. **Father, divinely electrify me!**

   Father, today I ask you to divinely electrify me with your glorious power and anointing so that I may impart gifts and graces of the spirit into the life of those I come in contact with, so that they may be established and made strong and your name glorified, in Jesus' name. Amen!

About the Author

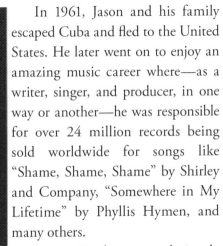

In 1961, Jason and his family escaped Cuba and fled to the United States. He later went on to enjoy an amazing music career where—as a writer, singer, and producer, in one way or another—he was responsible for over 24 million records being sold worldwide for songs like "Shame, Shame, Shame" by Shirley and Company, "Somewhere in My Lifetime" by Phyllis Hymen, and many others.

In 1977, he was gloriously converted, and he entered into full-time ministry in 1982. Dr. Alvarez led praise and worship for R.W. Schambach and Nicky Cruz and later served as a music minister with Pastor Dave Demola.

Now Dr. Jason Alvarez pastors one of the most dynamic churches on the East Coast, The Love of Jesus Family Church in Orange, New Jersey, and oversees churches and ministries around the world.

Please share this book with someone else and
email me if it has helped you in any way.

Jalvarez1251@gmail.com

For booking information, my music, and
teaching CDs, call 973-676-4200.

My music is also available at iTunes, Amazon, and Jamm.org.

Send your special prayer requests and donations to:
Jason Alvarez Ministries
448 Highland Ave.
Orange, NJ 07050

Love you much!

Printed in the United States
By Bookmasters